Social Consciousness and Career Awareness:
Emerging Link in Higher Education

by John S. Swift, Jr.

ASHE-ERIC Higher Education Report No. 8, 1990

Prepared by

Clearinghouse on Higher Education
The George Washington University

In cooperation with

Association for the Study
of Higher Education

Published by

School of Education and Human Development
The George Washington University

Jonathan D. Fife, Series Editor

Cite as
Swift, John S. Jr. 1990. *Social Consciousness and Career Awareness: Emerging Link in Higher Education.* ASHE-ERIC Higher Education Report No. 8. Washington, D.C.: The George Washington University, School of Education and Human Development.

Library of Congress Catalog Card Number 91-65607
ISSN 0884-0040
ISBN 1-878380-05-2

Managing Editor: Bryan Hollister
Manuscript Editor: Katharine Bird
Cover design by Michael David Brown, Rockville, Maryland

The ERIC Clearinghouse on Higher Education invites individuals to submit proposals for writing monographs for the *ASHE-ERIC Higher Education Report* series. Proposals must include:
1. A detailed manuscript proposal of not more than five pages.
2. A chapter-by-chapter outline.
3. A 75-word summary to be used by several review committees for the initial screening and rating of each proposal.
4. A vita and a writing sample.

ERIC **Clearinghouse on Higher Education**
School of Education and Human Development
The George Washington University
One Dupont Circle, Suite 630
Washington, DC 20036-1183

This publication was prepared partially with funding from the Office of Educational Research and Improvement, U.S. Department of Education, under contract no. ED RI-88-062014. The opinions expressed in this report do not necessarily reflect the positions or policies of OERI or the Department.

EXECUTIVE SUMMARY

Authors of some educational reports written during the 1980s think contemporary college students lack exposure to citizenship and concern for others. The same authors think that the education young people receive does not teach them how to serve as involved citizens. Finally, the authors are convinced that the way to teach these vital matters is by making a period of volunteer service part of the college experience (Boyer 1986; Newman 1985).

What Is Higher Education's Responsibility?

Higher education's historical responsibility has been to educate people to be leaders and providers for the welfare of society (Rudolph 1962). Colleges and universities have said that one of their missions is service. But the creation and support of service programs by educational institutions is limited to date. Faculty often are thought of as unwilling to become involved in such activities, and administrators often fail to see the benefits for their institutions from service. There are, however, benefits for faculty and institutions by providing volunteer service programs (Astin 1987).

Are College Students Selfish?

A major reason educators want contemporary youths to volunteer is due to their apparent selfishness: Many attend college primarily to prepare to enter the job market. Students appear preoccupied with status, money, and power. They seem focused on getting ahead and have little interest in changing the conditions around them. They consider solving the problems of society the responsibility of government (Astin, Green, and Korn 1987). But the concern students have for themselves may reflect more than selfishness. It may reflect their reaction to the economic, political, and social times they live in today.

Does Society Give Money and Time to Help Others?

Researchers report that individuals give the greatest amount of money to support nonprofit organizations. But the amount of money given is not increasing as fast as the need. Individual support of volunteer organizations is lagging while the expectation that government and/or business will do so is growing (Pifer 1987).

Individuals also are depended upon to volunteer to assist others. While a majority of people believe it is the obligation

108191

of every citizen to give and do as much as each can, less than half do either. Of those who do give and volunteer, the greater their involvement in their communities, the more they donate and serve (Hodgkinson and Weitzman 1988).

What Do Students Think About Volunteering?

A recent Gallup Poll on the value of voluntary national service found that 87 percent of those aged 18 to 24 believe it would be good for such a program to exist. Previous surveys have also found that a majority of young people favor a period of volunteer service, with 55 percent supporting conscription. Support of a period of service by youth also is favored by adults (Dolan 1986; National Service Secretariat 1988b).

Students who participate in volunteer programs report that the experience provides a variety of positive rewards. These include: knowledge, self-confidence, information about specific careers or academic majors, appreciation for being participatory citizens, and the opportunity to give back to society some of what society has given to them.

Student volunteers believe that their peers also would like the opportunity to volunteer. They do not believe that their generation is selfish. Rather, they believe that the problem lies in the inability of young people to find ways to serve society. They feel that service programs are needed (Fitch 1987).

Will Congress Legislate National Service?

Concern that youths need a service experience is great enough among Democratic legislators that in 1989 they introduced 20 bills to create a national service program. In addition, President Bush has proposed a national volunteer program. While his proposal includes no incentives, it also does not tie the receipt of financial aid to providing one or two years of service. Some proposed legislation requires those seeking financial aid to volunteer as a condition for aid (Kuntz 1989).

Any service program would need to be funded. One proposal for funding under consideration is to alter current federal budget line items including monies now going to education. Because some are convinced that students who serve should be rewarded, proposals for rewards include the granting of vouchers to pay for college education. The fund's source to pay those who serve could be the current financial aid programs in which at least one proposal would be eliminated.

Higher education is concerned about the potential impact changes in funding and the requirement of service will have. Some programs being conceived include requiring service for a one or two year period before a young person enters college. At the extreme, the impact could be significant; even a limited national service program will effect higher education (Danzig and Szanton 1986).

What Actions Should Higher Education Take?

Colleges and universities should take the lead in teaching youths about civic responsibility.

1. Curricular changes should be considered to teach youths the skills and knowledge needed to be participatory citizens.
2. Youths need opportunities to put classroom learning into practice. Students need service programming so they can volunteer, be exposed to social problems, and have the opportunity to solve those problems (MacArthur 1985).
3. Higher education should support altering the Federal Work-Study Program to provide opportunities for students to earn while serving others (Eberly and Sherraden 1982a; Newman 1985).
4. Programs need to be developed on campus, and/or with nonprofit agencies so students can participate in community service (Boyer 1986).

Service programming will require funding, and it is to the benefit of colleges and universities to seek support from foundations, individuals, and the government to create programs and new courses and to restructure the curriculum. Restructuring and the creation of new programs also means that faculty and staff need to become involved as participatory citizens. Faculty set examples, as do administrators.

Some colleges and universities, recognizing the need for a period of service for youth and the need for programs, have created both. National organizations have formed to facilitate student volunteers; for example, the Campus Outreach Opportunity League, a student organized group with chapters on 450 campuses. Another is the Campus Compact, an organization of 140 colleges and universities working under the direction of the Education Commission of the States. Both organizations provide a variety of services and support for institutions to create and operate volunteer service programs (Theus 1988).

ADVISORY BOARD

CONSULTING EDITORS

Brenda M. Albright
State of Tennessee Higher Education Commission

Walter R. Allen
University of California

Louis W. Bender
Florida State University

William E. Becker
Indiana University

Rita Bornstein
University of Miami

Paul T. Brinkman
National Center for Higher Education Management Systems

David G. Brown
University of North Carolina–Asheville

Robert F. Carbone
University of Maryland

David W. Chapman
State University of New York–Albany

Jay L. Chronister
University of Virginia

Linda Clement
University of Maryland

Richard A. Couto
Tennessee State University

Mildred Garcia
Montclair State College

Edward R. Hines
Illinois State University

Don Hossler
Indiana University

William Ihlanfeldt
Northwestern University

Greg Johnson
Harvard College

Jeanne M. Likens
Ohio State University

Dierdre A. Ling
University of Massachusetts

Jerry W. Miller
American College Testing

James R. Mingle
State Higher Education Executive Officers

Richard W. Moore
California State University–Northridge

Richard Morrill
Centre College

C. Gail Norris
Utah System of Education, State Board of Regents

Robert L. Payton
Indiana University

Joseph F. Phelan
University of New Hampshire

Laura I. Rendón
North Carolina State University

Charles U. Smith
Florida Agricultural and Mechanical University

Sharon P. Smith
Princeton University

Susan Stroud
Brown University

REVIEW PANEL

Charles Adams
University of Massachusetts–Amherst

Richard Alfred
University of Michigan

Philip G. Altbach
State University of New York at Buffalo

Louis C. Attinasi, Jr.
University of Houston

Ann E. Austin
Vanderbilt University

Robert J. Barak
Iowa State Board of Regents

Alan Bayer
Virginia Polytechnic Institute and State University

John P. Bean
Indiana University

Louis W. Bender
Florida State University

Carol Bland
University of Minnesota

Deane G. Bornheimer
New York University

John A. Centra
Syracuse University

Arthur W. Chickering
George Mason University

Jay L. Chronister
University of Virginia

Mary Jo Clark
San Juan Community College

Shirley M. Clark
Oregon State System of Higher Education

Darrel A. Clowes
Virginia Polytechnic Institute and State University

CONTENTS

FOREWORD

Historically, volunteer citizen participation has played a major part in our country and in our higher education institutions. Up until the mid nineteen hundreds, the majority of our social services were provided by volunteer organizations such as the fraternal and religious organizations that helped to maintain services for the poor, homes for the elderly, and higher education for the intellectually thirsty. More recently, there has been increasing concern over the lack of emphasis on the value of civic participation in all areas of our society, and especially in the school systems.

A number of conditions have led to the current, inadequate level of volunteerism. Since the late 1930s, government at all levels has taken a major role in the control, management and support of social services. Because of the vastness of this support, individuals perceive that there is less need for their volunteer efforts. Since even earlier in this century, there has been a general agreement that education should be value-free. As the Scientific Model became predominant, emphasis on moral concerns diminished.

The increasing size of our society, the rapidity of change, and the general high pace of our lives have caused many individuals to develop a sense of impotency. They sense that their actions would have little impact overall. The changing economy of the 1980s provided further impetus for the decline of volunteerism. The reduction in disposable income forced both parents in some families to hold jobs in order to maintain a minimal standard of living. The prosperity of the eighties encouraged other individuals and couples to work even harder in order to achieve an even higher level of income. The 'yuppies' are generally symbolic of that group, especially the sub-group labeled DINKs, standing for Double Income, No Kids (they want it all and don't want to share it).

At the same time, the economics of the eighties have brought a renewed awareness of the need for citizen participation. As federal support was decreased for local social programs and as individuals became increasingly dissatisfied with the meaninglessness of their more materialistic lifestyles, many concerned people began looking to educational institutions to promote social awareness.

There are several fundamental reasons why higher education must demonstrate more concern for infusing the value of social awareness into their students. One way or another, a large portion of the end use of knowledge—be it the humanities, science or general career development—eventually relates to our society. Connecting this knowledge more directly to social programs that emphasize volunteer action could only help to bring more real world awareness to the education process.

Value-free education is basically a false concept: Education is actually a value-laden activity. To not recognize this consciously and to not incorporate these values into the curriculum would dilute the total impact of the education process. As our society and higher education become more aware of humankind's impact on the natural environment, they are also becoming more aware in general of the impact of our social environment on the individual. This awareness is gradually being integrated into the higher education curriculum. Finally, as higher education institutions experience increasing financial restraints, there will be an increasing need for institutions to develop programs encouraging student participation activities that help to decrease institution expenses.

In his report, John S. Swift, Jr., program director of the College Level Examination Program of the College Board Programs Division at Educational Testing Service, reviews the current literature and data on the volunteerism role of higher education. He discusses higher education's historical responsibility; the characteristics and desires of contemporary college students; the economic, social and personal aspects of volunteering; the actions already taken to create local and national service programs; and the roles and actions necessary for higher education in the future.

"Volunteerism," "citizen participation," "personal involvement in our social environment;" call it what you will, it is fundamental to a successfully functioning society. The general purpose of higher education is to develop basic knowledge and a sense of self that will empower an individual to make a positive contribution to society. If the academic and extracurricular programs of higher education place greater emphasis on volunteer student participation, this empowerment will only be enhanced.

Jonathan D. Fife
Series Editor, Professor and
Director, ERIC Clearinghouse on Higher Education

A CALL FOR HIGHER EDUCATION
TO PROVIDE VOLUNTEER OPPORTUNITIES

In 1989 more than 20 bills were introduced in Congress and President Bush unveiled his plan to create some type of volunteer service corps (DeLoughry and Myers 1989; Ivory 1989; and Kuntz 1989). The number of bills in a single year is unusual, but the desire to create a service program is not. No fewer than 35 bills have been presented to Congress in the last 23 years.

Educators who are calling for reform think that higher education prepares youths to enter the job market but not to enter society as involved citizens.

Historically, higher education has provided students with opportunities to practice citizenship and to show concern for the welfare of others (Rudolph 1962). College students of the 1980s, however, are seen as lacking that exposure. Consequently, U.S. legislators, educators, and business leaders have joined together to form the Coalition for National Service. Its members are concerned about what they perceive as a lack of civic responsibility on the part of today's college youth.

The coalition includes U.S. legislators such as California Representative Leon Panetta, educators such as Harvard University's Derek Bok, and business leaders such as pollster George Gallup, Jr (Coalition for National Service 1988, pp. 27–29).

A Call for Student Volunteers

The number of bills to create corps of volunteers is not without a parallel in education. The 1980s may be remembered as a time when more reports called for educational reform than ever before.

One reform being called for is to introduce students to ". . . the responsibilities of citizenship in a democracy" (National Commission on the Role and Future of State Colleges and Universities 1986, p. 10). The reform's purpose is to "develop within each student a sense of country and community service and a desire to help others" (Newman 1985, p. 39). This will "help students see that they are not only autonomous individuals but also members of a larger community to which they are accountable" (Boyer 1986, p. 218).

Educators who are calling for reform think that higher education prepares youths to enter the job market but not to enter society as involved citizens. They view students as products of an educational system that fails to encourage civic participation inside or.outside the classroom (Boyer 1986; Newman 1985; the National Commission on the Role and Future of

State Colleges and Universities 1986).

Too many college students are seen as lacking knowledge of historical facts, failing to understand how a democracy exists, and showing little interest in the U.S. political system (Giroux 1987; Hepburn 1985). Reformers think that this lack of knowledge, understanding, and interest results in students who are neither sensitive to the needs of others nor interested in being active citizens. They are convinced that college students need

> *opportunities to participate in public and community service activities as part of their undergraduate experience. Institutional encouragement of students to take advantage of such opportunities benefits society as a whole by extending education, by inducing individual participation in the political process, and by enhancing student understanding of the general welfare* (National Commission on the Role and Future of State Colleges and Universities 1986, p. 10).

Authors of reports calling for students to become involved civically think that educational reform includes colleges and universities accepting an active role in providing public service opportunities. To accomplish this goal, proposals include the suggestion that college students volunteer their time to assist others (Bok 1986; Kennedy 1986; Moskos 1988).

To understand the reformers' desire for students to become involved in serving others, it is necessary to know what is meant by "volunteerism." While there are different interpretations, the following definitions are provided for use in this monograph.

Volunteerism Defined

Volunteerism may be defined in three ways, according to George K. Floro. His first and second definitions are appropriate here.

> *Life-sharing volunteerism is the one most directly associated with experiential learning and mutual benefits to both volunteer and recipient. The justification for doing the work . . . is enjoyment. Satisfactions come from the job or workplace, the participation with others who do it, and from the work itself—the sense of achievement from one's own labor. . . . Another characteristic of this type is that the resources*

of goodwill and information are readily renewable social resources.

The second type is identified as the protection and reform type. The major purpose is to protect or preserve what is cherished. Here is where the sacrifice and the altruism linked with it are to be seen. The social resources may not be renewable, as when one (a volunteer) gives one's own life for a friend. . . . What is done or expressed is justified by love or outrage in behalf of who or what is threatened. The attention is steadfastly upon the victim(s)—persons, groups, or the cherished principle or belief (Floro 1985, p. 166).

A term that some people may confuse with volunteerism is *philanthropy.* For this monograph's purposes, philanthropy is

essentially sponsorship . . . a catalyst. Sponsorship is support, financial and/or social network in nature, of those people, programs, projects, etc., engaged on the frontier of voluntarism—to provide direct service, to bring about institutional change, or at least to do what needs to be done to improve or enrich life (Floro 1985, p. 165).

Sponsorship has brought individuals together to assist others. This has resulted in the creation of organizations and agencies to carry out voluntary activities. The number of nonprofit institutions has increased, and they now encompass all aspects of society (O'Connell 1982). There are so many such organizations that in 1978 two groups, the Coalition of National Voluntary Organizations and the National Council on Philanthropy, merged to create the "independent sector" (Gardner 1983).

The independent sector, also called the "third sector" (in contrast with the first and second sectors of business and government), includes organizations and agencies which are nonprofit in charter and by tax law. Business is thought of as the for-profit sector of society while government is thought of as the sector that provides for and protects society.

Many of society's expectations of the independent sector are similar to those it has of education. This should not be surprising because nonprofit agencies that are dependent on volunteers and institutions of higher education have a great deal in common. Both groups exist to serve somewhat idealistic purposes, deliver services, and have goals that often are difficult to measure.

To some extent both groups rely on philanthropy, a positive community spirit, and a supportive political climate. It seems that nonprofit agencies and colleges and universities should be natural allies (Greenberg 1982).

If third sector organizations and educational institutions are natural allies they could benefit one another (see chap. 5). Higher education could use the independent sector as a source of volunteer opportunities for students. It also could provide a number of services that would assist third sector organizations. After all, colleges and universities have held a leadership role in the education of society.

Higher Education: Its Historical Responsibility

Has higher education had the historical responsibility to prepare people to be involved citizens? Founders of the early colonial colleges may not have written their goals as institutional mission statements, but they had them.

> *In retrospect, they seem clear enough: to train not only the clergy but also a new educational leadership; to combat the restlessness of youth in a developing country; to instill in their students piety, loyalty, and responsible citizenship; and to transmit knowledge that would be useful, not merely in the classical sense of preparing gentlemen, but for the practical demands of a changing world* (Boyer and Hechinger 1981, p. 9).

Placing emphasis on having an educated society was no accident. It was thought that without education society would be barbaric; with it, society would be civilized. Until well into the 19th century the college experience was primarily an opportunity for "broad social purpose." The social purpose included providing leadership to solve political problems, offering a community where people of similar persuasion could share common concerns, and meeting societal needs rather than the goals of individuals (Rudolph 1962).

Society's changing expectations

But as the 19th century ended, the expectations American society had of higher education changed. Emphasis on colleges and universities serving society, preparing the leaders, and being primarily concerned with the welfare of a majority all decreased. Colleges became more focused on the expectations of their students and less on those of society, and their graduates discovered that a college education was more important as a personal investment and less as a social investment (Rudolph 1962, p. 65).

Realizing that a majority of people were neither attending college nor appearing to benefit from the public support colleges were given, Congress passed the Morrill Act in 1862. A major purpose of the Act was to create state colleges that would serve the broader needs of society, including agriculture and technology, and to welcome a more diverse student constituency than was entering the private colleges.

Society looked to the state universities where the traditional collegiate education was being transformed to one meant for all and in the process also became more democratic. In addition to offering an education to all, the public universities tried to add a commitment to the idea of public service (Rudolph 1962, p. 286).

Thus, while the early colleges were founded to educate people to serve society, over the last one hundred years colleges and universities have come to serve diverse purposes, to accept the individualism of society, and to educate people so they may become successful in their own terms (Giroux 1987; Newman 1985). This diversity of purpose has resulted in a complex educational system; a system that is viewed as having given up its public service responsibility as a primary function.

Now, however, many reformers think that the public service function should be revived and students should become involved in volunteering.

Higher Education's Role in Volunteer Programming

For faculty and staff to alter current curricular offerings, put new programs in place, and become involved in volunteer programming, they must believe that there are positive reasons to participate. Involvement by higher education has been limited.

The universities and colleges have a dismal record as providers of community resources and services. Endowed with a plentiful supply of trained researchers and student workers, the universities have the skilled manpower volun-

tary organizations are seeking. Their new rhetoric for com-
munity involvement and public service has not been
matched by any collective commitment to action from the
administration, faculty, or indeed, student level. At the very
moment when they are most needed to provide community
services, they are either unprepared or unwilling to respond
to the challenge (Eisenberg 1977, p. 861).

Eisenberg's view of higher education's involvement in providing community service is disheartening. While he states
a condition, that condition has not always existed. Colleges
and universities have served society and their responsibility
has not diminished.

Altruistically, higher education has a responsibility to be
involved with public service because of its unique position
of being the center of knowledge; it has an obligation to
share its knowledge with more than its own students and
faculty. From the position of intellectual self-interest, public
service provides a laboratory for testing current knowledge.
Putting knowledge into practice permits discovery of what
is still unknown, what works, and what does not.

  Finally, higher education is obligated to help society as
a repayment for its financial support. Because both private
and public institutions receive direct and indirect tax sup-
port, they have a responsibility for more than just teaching
and conducting research (Crosson 1983, p. 14).

The reasons for institutional involvement in providing service that Crosson gives are more far reaching than those
sought by the educational reformers who seek service programming to involve youth in volunteering. Their concern
focuses on today's youth, not just on the responsibilities of
the colleges and universities. Reasons given to institute volunteer programs include:

- concern over the apparent growth of individualism
- the isolation of the students of the 1980s
- higher education has had as its mission the preparation
  of the leaders of society
- education was, at least in part, created to educate a pop-
  ulace in order to preserve a democratic form of government (Boyer 1986; Campus Compact 1987; National Com-

mission on the Role and Future of State Colleges and Universities 1986).

Why conflict exists

In part, the conflict between those who would have citizenship a primary purpose of education and those who would let students seek what they want lies in understanding individualism in a democratic society. Individualism is needed for a free and creative society, and historically the strength of the U.S. democracy is in the commitment to personal improvement and fulfillment. Individualism is necessary, but so is sensitivity to selfishness.

It is appropriate, therefore, for educational institutions that are preparing students to be citizens in a participatory democracy to understand the dilemmas and paradoxes of an individualistic culture (Boyer 1986, p.68).

A balance is needed between the individual's goals and the obligation each person has for society. And "through an effective college education students should become personally empowered and also committed to the common good" (Boyer 1986, p. 69).

Public service through volunteerism is a way for higher education to return something tangible to those who often feel they support it without any direct benefit. Through volunteer programs colleges and universities can demonstrate willingness to engage in helping people who normally do not fall within the purview of the institution. And students can be seen in a positive light rather than one that often categorizes them negatively (Balderston 1978; Ventresca et al. 1987).

How student volunteers help

A student volunteer offered this observation about positive reactions of the community towards college students after they became involved in service programming.

I've found you can change your university's image in a community. The community always viewed us as the kids who move into the apartments in the neighborhoods; who stay up late and play their stereos; and who go to the bathroom on their cars. Changing our university's image in the community has been one of the really good things we've

---

done. Instead of saying, 'There's those rich, loud, arrogant college kids,' we've been able to impress people with our honesty and sincerity (Newman 1987, p. 27).

In addition to changing the image an institution may have in the community, Crosson maintains that service can assist students to develop "ideas of value" and deal with the concepts of individualism and community (1983, p. 14).

During the 1960s and 1970s, several urban problems developed: urban blight, high unemployment, high crime, shortages of housing, inadequate educational facilities, inadequate medical facilities, and a lack of effective urban planning (Mayville 1980). Urban institutions committed themselves to helping solve these problems as part of their service missions (Crosson 1983).

Student service can include developing solutions to real-world problems when students become involved in internships and other practical experiences while continuing their formal education and preparing for their roles as professional and concerned citizens.

Faculty also become involved in solving social problems through consulting and other activities. Institutions of higher education can join with government, communities, agencies, and other constituencies to effect "efforts to apply scientific and technical knowledge to complex social problems" (Crosson 1983, pp. 15–16).

What Crosson says can be interpreted as idealistic, or it can be accepted as a possibility on the sincerity of providing service programming. But current service programs need to be expanded and/or created to achieve the benefits just discussed.

Service and the college agenda
While the service function is an integral part of most college and university agendas, it often exists as part of academic units rather than as part of separate offices created specifically for that purpose. Few such offices have the sole purpose of delivering public services. Most of the time it is presumed that public service missions will be carried out by existing administrative and academic units. The result can be a lack of attention to current needs, the provision of services that are not adequate, and a failure to recognize potential service opportunities (Crosson 1983, pp. 95–96).

Colleges and universities have created some centers which provide services to the community. Such centers often are designated as "research centers" and "continuing education centers." The concept of a centralized office of public service is usually just that, a concept. A few institutions and some systems have developed such an office, but generally they do not exist. Thus, the service function falls to individual units within the college or university (Crosson 1983).

On many college campuses "student affairs practitioners are often responsible for coordinating community service organizations and promoting volunteer service among college students" (Fitch 1987, p. 424).

Student groups and service opportunities. A variety of student groups can be found on most college campuses. Whether organized through residence halls, fraternities and sororities, or other organizations, these groups offer a starting place to create programs for students to volunteer. But the use of existing groups, as well as the creation of new programming, needs the support of the entire institution (Boyer 1986; Theus 1988). In the case of new programming, additional resources may need to be committed by the institution. Financial resources, as people involved with education know, are a concern. But involvement should not be predicated on financial remuneration alone. It should rest on educational values, quality of leadership, and institutional commitment to social responsibility (Eisenberg 1977) for the educational and societal benefits appear to outweigh the costs (Kennedy 1986).

While the creation and operation of a volunteer program may require additional financial resources, those costs can be partially or completely funded from external sources. This may be achieved through grants, community or agency support, foundation funding, and through financial aid—especially work-study.

Faculty, Staff, and Institutional Involvement

While colleges and universities give commitment to service functions, the attraction for faculty to participate in service activities is limited, if only because the reward structure often does not place the same emphasis on service that it does on teaching and research (Crosson 1983). And yet if students are to become volunteers, they need faculty and staff to support and/or to participate in voluntary service programs. But faculty and staff often are thought of as unwilling to become involved (Boyer 1986).

College faculty are caught in the crossfire of conflicting signals about the priorities of their work. On some campuses the pressure for scholarship is intense, while at the same time departmental commitments, classroom preparation and teaching, and students' need for academic guidance consume large amounts of time (Carnegie Foundation for the Advancement of Teaching 1985, pp. 33–34).

While it is suggested that faculty and staff have neither the time nor the interest to provide services as volunteers, many are willing to do so. These individuals see their roles as more than classroom instructors and researchers. They are committed to their jobs, enjoy their responsibilities as teachers, and generously give of their time outside the classroom to assist the undergraduates (Boyer 1986, p. 119).

While some faculty are busy with teaching, research, and other activities that do not emphasize service, others are involved with students outside the classroom in service activities. Such participation may be the result of desire to be with students, concern for social conditions, or because such involvement is a benefit professionally. Faculty from some disciplines may participate because service activities are part of the formal education they are teaching to students.

While not all faculty may benefit from participating in the service function, there are several possible benefits for faculty and staff who become involved in volunteer programs including:

1. Faculty who become directly involved can serve as role models and leaders for students. This could provide them with the student attention that some feel they are losing (McCartan 1988, p. 20).
2. Participation can provide access to new research opportunities. This can provide additional resources for faculty pressured to carry out scholarly activities.
3. Consulting opportunities can develop through contacts made by faculty members (Bowen and Schuster 1986, pp. 19–20).
4. Volunteer programs may provide exciting alternatives to

traditional classroom instruction. Participation by faculty in volunteer service could provide them with "laboratory" situations from which they could do research and expand their knowledge. Their participation could place them ". . . in a position of a learner" (Torralba 1988, p. 4). They could then return to their classrooms with current and/ or new information to alter their course content.

While not all faculty will desire to participate in volunteer service, more may be interested if the current pressure for research as the major method to determine reward is balanced by placing equal concern on other activities. Many educational reformers think that faculty should be expected to participate in public service (Bernstein 1985).

Faculty who become directly involved can serve as role models and leaders for students.

Creating Volunteer Service Programming

Faculty, staff, and institutions can reap rewards for supporting and participating in student volunteer programs. Providing activities to educate students about democracy, social service, and leadership responsibilities would return higher education to its historical role—serving society by educating leaders (Boyer 1986; National Commission on the Role and Future of State Colleges and Universities 1986).

Currently colleges and universities are not viewed as taking a leadership role in exposing students to service opportunities. That is one purpose of the 20 bills presented to Congress during 1989: to revive the tradition of exposing students to broad social experiences.

Nunn-McCurdy bill

Among the bills, the Nunn-McCurdy bill stands out due to its controversial requirements regarding financial aid. Specifically, the bill would require national service of all students who want financial aid (see chap. 4). A change in how financial aid is given would have an impact on higher education. It could be a change that would affect the way colleges and universities do business.

It appears to be in the best interest of higher education to take the lead and address the concern that students are self-interested. This does not mean institutions have to be pioneers. Many institutions have programs in place. Colleges and universities can tap into existing opportunities, as many have. These opportunities could include creating on-campus centers to assist students to volunteer; joining the Campus Compact or the Campus Outreach Opportunity League; aligning with other colleges and universities to assist students to do community service; and offering other service orientated activities and programs.

CONTEMPORARY COLLEGE STUDENTS:
Characteristics and Desires

Environmental and Economic Conditions

From the 1940s through the 1960s students were committed to larger goals and purposes. They were willing to interact with society, accept its values, and shoulder civic responsibilities. The students of the 1950s and 1960s saw their parents' economic prosperity flourish. They were told they could achieve even more by working hard and earning a college degree. Students who followed those instructions achieved upward mobility and financial prosperity. Then, what society promised and what could be achieved were equivalent (Guardo 1982, pp. 500–502).

In the mid-1960s students were in transition. In the late 1960s and early 1970s they were seen as radicals, activists, and uncommitted to accepting social values. The students of the mid-1970s were seen as narcissistic and withdrawn from society, shunning institutional norms and social commitments. But by the mid- to late-1970s students had again entered a period of transition. In the early 1980s social upheavals lessened and they returned to accepting the values of society (Guardo 1982; Thompson 1985).

Students in the 1990s are concerned with financial security. They fear they will not have the same opportunities to achieve economically and socially what their parents achieved (Kennedy 1986; Wagner 1987). Students are living through numerous social changes, including "a turbulent economy . . . a tough job market . . . international tensions, terrorism, and the threat of nuclear war" (Levine 1986, p. 3). They are seeking stability, security, and the opportunity to pursue their dreams as preceding generations have done (Bok 1986).

Social changes are thought to contribute to contemporary students being selfish. But it may be that they are realistic in their thinking, their goals, and their actions. Students are called self-centered, isolated, passive, materialistic, and conformist. At the same time, it appears there are reasons for them to focus on themselves and to use their educational opportunities to prepare for jobs offering financial rewards. If they think that they cannot change events around them, there is little reason to seek to be involved (Thompson 1985).

The college graduates of the 1980s represent part of the first American generation the members of which, "by and large, will not have access to the economic advantages afforded their parents" (Kennedy 1986, p. 3).

Social and Political Conditions

If economic conditions are not enough to cause today's students to focus on themselves, the political system also contributes to their apparent self-serving actions. "The legacy of the Great Society has been tempered by more realistic expectations of what government can accomplish" (Hartle and Taylor 1985, p. 53). President Reagan's popularity with college students centered on his views of economic "growth and job opportunity . . . no-nonsense ideas about foreign affairs . . . [and] a military build-up while calling for more action on arms control" (Hartle and Taylor 1985, p. 53).

Problems students encountered in the 1980s included AIDS, the Iran affair, dealings with the Contras, hostages in the Middle East, the growing use of drugs, environmental catastrophes, as well as

> *whatever else might [be] on the newscast today to confront, challenge, and virtually overwhelm any sense of individual influence, impact, or control. The only seeming locus of control is oneself and those close to self. Thus, it makes sense that personal relationships are more salient to this student generation and that there is a preference for what is small and controllable in the world of work as well* (Guardo 1982, p. 502).

Becoming sensitive and flexible to the needs and demands of others has been replaced by students' focusing on their personal role in society (Thompson 1985). Achieving their personal role raises questions of whether students are willing to alter their opinions, dirty themselves by taking action to cause change, and learn about past events that continue to effect present social conditions.

It appears that the current positive tone set by government, and the willingness of college students to support and accept the rhetoric of the Reagan and Bush administrations creates situations in which students find it easy to accept the current social, economic, and political environments without question or concern (Hepburn 1985). This perceived acceptance of the status quo without being willing to get involved to cause change or to even voice concern over situations that previous generations would not have accepted is part of the reason people look for ways to involve today's students in service programs to foster civic participation.

Financial Conditions

Economic, political, and social events are only part of the reason youth of today are more focused on themselves. The financial conditions youth face today include the cost of a college education, inflation, and the cost of the basic necessities they want (or perceive they need).

Many students are financing part, or all, of their college expenses. Having to finance their education causes students to focus on two factors affecting their immediate condition: (1) financial; (2) work (Evangelauf 1987a; McCartan 1988).

According to the results of a survey commissioned by the Carnegie Foundation for the Advancement of Teaching in 1984, more than 62 percent of college students today work (McCartan 1988, p. 11). Why do so many college students hold jobs?

- More students are bearing the burden for all of their college costs.
- The current generation sees their material needs differently than those before them.
- Many students report that working provides more than financial benefits. They cite the opportunities of developing self-confidence, learning to manage time, making new friends, and enjoyment.

While faculty express concern about the amount of time students spend working, a researcher who compared working students with non-working students

found little difference between the two groups in the frequency with which they participated in such activities as reading for pleasure, volunteer services, attending parties, art exhibits, and cultural activities (McCartan 1988, p. 16).

If more students work more hours, and if their participation in service activities is no different than their contemporaries who do not work, the question of whether students have time for service may be a secondary issue. That is, rather than focus on the amount of work students do, institutions may need to focus on their policies and how to deal with this contemporary situation (McCartan 1988, pp. 11–17).

How students pay for higher education

Employment is one source used by students to pay for educational expenses. Financial aid is another source. An increasing part of that financial aid is loans. In 1986 the mean debt of graduates of public colleges was $6,685; for private college graduates, it was $8,950; and the average amount is rising (Evangelauf 1987a, pp. 1, 18).

Changes in the rules governing educational loans include increasing the amount students can borrow to finance under-graduate, graduate, and professional education. The result appears to be a future generation of well-educated people heavily in debt. In addition to educational loans, graduates enter the consumer market and increase their debts through the purchase of hard goods. A growing number of college graduates owe a great deal of money and need adequate employment to earn the amount required to pay their loans and bills. As a result, they may have decreased time for and interest in civic participation (Bok 1986; Evangelauf 1987a).

A possible solution to the dual problems of students work-ing and students borrowing more is to restructure the federal work-study program to make more funds available to support students who work in third sector agency positions.

Data/Characteristics of College Students

The observations of a number of individuals are the source for the summary of students enrolled in higher education dur-ing the 1980s presented in this chapter. Those views are the result of research done of students. A comparison of student attitudes and values from the last two decades can be made using data collected by the Cooperative Institutional Research Program (CIRP).

Each year 500,000 freshmen who are enrolled full time at 550 two- and four-year colleges and universities complete a questionnaire that is used to gather data, information, and opinions on a wide variety of issues, concerns, interests, and characteristics of succeeding classes (Astin, Green, and Korn 1987, p. 7).

Freshmen choice of majors

Freshmen selection of majors demonstrates the changes that have taken place over the last 20 years.

Business. Selection of majors demonstrates what many have said: Business is the most attractive program of study offered by colleges and universities today. Almost 22 percent of fresh-men choose this major. Their interest in business studies is supported by the doubling of the number of college freshmen planning to pursue business careers.

Engineering and computer science. Career interests in engineering and computer science also have increased, although 1983 marked the high point of such interest.

Education. Careers in education have experienced the greatest decline of interest, 71 percent over the last 20 years. Some recent signs, however, indicate that the trend may be reversing itself.

Helping professions. Occupations traditionally considered "the helping professions" have experienced declines of more than 50 percent. These include social work, ministry, nursing, and other health related jobs. The drop in interest seems related to two factors: Today's popular careers generally are high paying and do not require education beyond the bachelor's degree. Careers out of favor often are low paying and require advanced education (Astin et al. 1987; Dodge 1990).

Freshmen goals

Freshmen embrace certain values and have specific goals in life. These include:

Financial rewards. One goal is to be "well off financially." Seventeen years ago 40 percent of freshmen listed this as a priority; more recently 75 percent listed this as a goal.

Philosophy of life. The goal with the greatest loss of interest is "to develop a meaningful philosophy of life." It dropped from being a goal of 82.9 percent of freshmen in 1967 to 40.8 percent in 1989.

Power and status. Values that have been embraced at a growing rate in the last 20 years along with financial rewards include power and status. Freshmen currently believe attending college is a means to "make more money." They seek power, authority over others, and recognition. The percentages speak for themselves.

• Only 28.6 percent desired to have administrative responsibility for others 20 years ago; now 43.6 percent do.

- To be well off financially is the goal of 75.4 percent today; in 1971 it was the goal of 39.1 percent.

Helping others. Helping others, promoting racial understanding, and cleaning up the environment are not considered attractive goals today (Astin et al. 1987; Dodge 1990). Freshmen do not consider influencing government, changing social values, and participating in community action as areas where they could have a strong influence or involvement.

- Participation in a community action program was an objective of 29.4 percent of the freshmen in 1970; of 23.3 percent in 1989.
- Cleaning up the environment was the goal of 42.9 percent of the freshmen in 1971; of 20.3 percent in 1985. In 1989, being involved in cleaning up the environment was a goal of 26.1 percent of freshmen.
- Of special interest is the fact that 22 years ago 68.5 percent of freshmen saw themselves helping someone in difficulty, while in 1989 the percent seeing themselves helping someone in difficulty had dropped to 59.7 percent.
- In 1985, 70.4 percent of freshmen said they had provided assistance as volunteers before entering college. But in 1989, that percent had slipped to 62 percent, and just 5.4 percent had volunteered six or more hours per week (Astin et al. 1987, pp. 96–98; and Dodge 1990, pp. A33–34).

It may appear that the freshmen of 1989 continue to demonstrate the self-centeredness of which they are accused. It seems, however, that a growing number were active in demonstrations before they matriculated, and expect to continue to become personally involved while in college. The percent of freshmen who participated in demonstrations was 36.7; a proportion that was greater than "those who reported being active in the late 1960s . . ." (Dodge 1990).

Lessons Learned from Students of the 1960s
Students' fears of, and concerns about, society have led them to focus on themselves and their material well-being. For higher education,

the materialism stands in striking contrast to the espoused (but not always operational) values of academic institu-

tions that claim a primary concern for intellectual discovery and learning (Green and Astin 1985, p. 48).

Changes in society are causing changes in youth, and unless we address the changes we may create the type of citizens we speak about when we categorize college students today (Kennedy 1986).

Some educators might act as advocates for a return to the social service activities of the 1960s. This is unlikely to happen, but it might be possible to introduce the students of today to the kinds of activities their predecessors undertook.

Mississippi case history

Many students took part in volunteer activities to improve social conditions in the 1960s. One place they went to provide services was Mississippi. There they worked in situations that for many were a shock. They assisted in summer freedom schools, voter registration, and other community projects. While the civil rights story of the 1960s is largely history, for participants the effort shaped their lives (Chalmers 1984, pp. 36–39).

Their continued commitment to civic action comes from an awareness of the persistence of poverty, racial prejudice, and a skepticism about government. Their commitment is exemplified by their taking every opportunity to serve society. This is a missing characteristic of contemporary college students. Attention to developing a career, the drive for power, and desire to dominate the top of their field or profession categorizes today's students (Chalmers 1984, pp. 36–39).

Effects of the Mississippi experience. Almost half the Mississippi volunteers pursued careers in law and other professions. They include administrators, educators, consultants, institute directors, film makers, authors, and urban planners. Success in their estimation is measured by social usefulness, not personal achievement. When they completed their formal education they often took positions in inner city locations. They went to work providing services in mental health, civil rights, corrections, and social work for those in need.

Today, many run the organizations, or similar ones, where they held their first jobs. Their activities as college students shaped their lifelong values. They left the comforts of their environments to serve others. Through the experiences of

Students' fears of, and concerns about, society have led them to focus on themselves and their material well-being.

volunteering their outlooks and career directions changed. Most consider themselves successful, and most are—even by the standards applied by college students of the 1980s (Chalmers 1984, pp. 36–39).

How Civic Participation Affects Students

How does participation in civic service programs affect college students? Does it increase their ability to work with others, respect for adults, attitudes towards authorities, personal and social responsibility, self-worth, and self-esteem in social situations?

Research indicates that students who participate change positively compared to those who do not, and in 14 of 28 areas the change is statistically significant. The greatest gains are in the areas of duty, competency, and social efficacy. The largest significant difference between the two groups is the sense of duty and social welfare orientation demonstrated by the students in experiential education programs (Hedin and Conrad 1980, p. 13).

What students say

The effects of volunteering show themselves in student reactions when questioned. In one study,

> *about 90 percent of student volunteers say service-learning experience was as valuable or more valuable to them than classroom work. Tutoring, for example, was found to increase significantly the empathy, altruism, and self-esteem of the tutor in addition to increasing his or her academic averages. Service also often has a positive impact on motivation, ability to choose a career, and smoothing the assumption of increasing responsibility* (Boyer 1986, p. 216).

Another study, completed in 1986, found that students thought volunteering provided a sense of satisfaction in helping others, caused an increase in concern for others, offered the chance to meet and make new friends, and was a way to learn new skills and an opportunity to return to society some of what society gives to them (Fitch 1987, pp. 427–29).

The first four recipients of the Robinson Student Humanitarian Achievement Award, given by the Campus Compact in recognition of humanitarian activities conducted for the benefit of society in 1987, consider their involvement as significant opportunities with lifelong implications. All four realize the extensive and diverse needs of society. They recognize that individually they make a difference, but when they join forces with other people the difference becomes much greater.

One recipient thinks that it is

a big misconception that college students are apathetic or self-centered. . . . The majority of them [students] really had such a lack of knowledge of what's going on in the outside world. It was ignorance, not self-centeredness, that kept them uninvolved (Newman 1987, p. 23).

The award recipients see fellow students as people without the knowledge to understand the needs of society and how to contribute to alleviate those needs. Civic participation by college students could be increased by knowing that each person could make a difference, by having institutional support, and with a national organization assisting students to contribute their time (Newman 1987).

The four feel that greater institutional support is needed to increase student participation in service programs. As a student observed:

You find a lack of encouragement from faculty as far as being involved in a process. And if they are unaware of what's going on, then they don't encourage students to get involved. A lot of times the administrators may give you smiles, but they don't actually go out and help you, and they pretty much leave it up to you to do it (Newman 1987, p. 24).

However, another recipient found that

we've made a lot of progress in getting support from the university and that's been really good in terms of what people can do. Just by the president of the university, or people from his office, or faculty saying 'we support what this group of people is trying to do,' it makes progress possible (Newman 1987, p. 24).

As those comments indicate, the four students' observations about their experiences as volunteers and their thoughts about their peers are positive. At question, though, is whether their peers on higher education campuses will become involved in volunteer activities.

VOLUNTEERING AND PHILANTHROPY:
Economic, Social, and Personal Aspects

Volunteering may be defined as giving one's time to provide service to another person. Philanthropy may be considered as giving one's money to support activities that provide services for others. Today, however, colleges and universities may have to find new resources to create service programs. Independent sector agencies also need resources to provide services. And while some people may believe that support will come from business and/or government, third sector agencies historically have received the majority of their financial support from individuals.

Economic and Financial Data from 1968 to 1985

The 1960-69 decade represented a period when the cumulative rise in giving was greater than the rise in the cost of living. In 1969 charitable giving was "at an all-time high—over $159.6 billion—and the proportion of the population that voluntarily contributes to charity [was] the highest ever" (O'Connell 1982, p. 19).[1]

Results of a 1974 study show $59.3 billion dollars were contributed that year, and $59.3 billion dollars worth of time was donated to charitable causes. In addition, government funds, endowment earnings, and tuition and fee payments were made to a variety of institutions. The total came to about **$189.8 billion dollars** worth of revenues for the nonprofit sector, or about half the amount spent on food in a year (Commission on Private Philanthropy and Public Needs 1975, p. 34).

Individual contributions

In 1980 giving from individuals totaled $56.7 billion dollars, or 1.84 percent of personal income; corporations gave $3.60 billion, or 1.05 percent of net pretax income. Foundations gave $3.4 billion the same year (Opinion Roundup 1982).

In 1984 an average of $650 was contributed by 89 percent of all Americans. This represented an average of 2.4 percent of their household incomes. "While more than half of all Americans gave less than 1 percent of their incomes to charities, more than one out of four gave 3 percent or more" (Yankelovich, Skelly, and White, Inc. 1986).

---

[1] All dollar figures given in this section have been adjusted to 1988 dollars using the Consumer Price Index.

But by 1987 the average contribution had dropped to $562.00 and was contributed by 71 percent of the population. And of the total amount given, 70 percent came from 19 percent of all the households (Hodgkinson and Weitzman 1988). In other words,

of the approximately $70.5 billion given annually now for charitable purposes by individual Americans—which is 82.7 percent of the total giving, since only 5.4 percent is donated by foundations, 5.4 percent by corporations, and 6.5 percent in the form of bequests—the great bulk is provided by people of quite ordinary means. In fact, over half of the $70.5 billion is given by people whose incomes fall in the bottom three-fifths of the income scale (Pifer 1987, p. 120).

Individuals provide the major share of the independent sector's financial support. But will individuals continue to believe they should support the independent sector? Or will they decide that business and/or government should do so?

Independent Sector

Expenditures by independent sector agencies and organizations totaled about $131 billion in 1985. This amount was five percent of the Gross National Product (GNP). The government is the largest source of support followed by various fees and dues charged, then by donations made by individuals, and, finally, by the gifts from foundations and corporations (Pifer 1987, p. 124).

Government funding has permitted the independent sector to grow, and thus provide increased benefits to society. But the government-independent sector partnership, and its positive results, are in jeopardy because government support has been reduced (Pifer 1987; Van Til 1985). While the Reagan administration talked a great deal about the need to increase civic participation by individuals, its support of the independent sector was not equal to what it asked the people of the United States to do.

From 1982 to 1985 . . . federal support for nonprofit organizations, exclusive of that provided through the big health-care programs, Medicare and Medicaid, dropped $17 billion below the level of 1980. Social service organizations lost $9 billion, or more than 35 percent of their federal aid. And *organizations concerned with housing and neighborhood improvement lost a similar percentage* (Pifer 1987, p. 125).

Some people think that the independent sector will not be able to sustain many of the activities it currently supports, while others think that business and industry will take over that role (Opinion Roundup 1982). The corporate sector has been the beneficiary of tax laws that support philanthropic activities. But what actions can and does this sector take to provide for social needs?

Corporate Sector

The expectation that the corporate sector will replace what the independent sector does is questionable. Corporate philanthropy was tied to a narrow definition of self-interest well into the 20th century. For a company to make a donation and have it tax deductible, the recipient had to serve the company's direct benefit. Corporate contributions had to meet the "direct benefit" rule until 1953 when "the Supreme Court of New Jersey . . . overturned the 'direct benefit' rule . . ." (Karl 1983, p. 134).

The change in rules restricting corporate giving was in part due to the recognition that new sources of support for the welfare of society had to be found. Individuals no longer could provide all the resources needed, and while government supported some social activities, needs outstripped resources. Consequently, the corporate sector was looked upon as a partial replacement for the individual (Karl 1983). However, corporate giving often has focused on specific activities.

> *The traditional role of the corporation in social problem solving has largely involved corporate philanthropy and employee volunteerism in local communities that are characterized as 'corporate good citizenship.' That role has involved financial contributions to selected educational, cultural, and welfare organizations, top-executive leadership in headquarters cities, and the development of benefit plans for the protection of employees, pensioners, and their families* (Steckmest 1982, p. 144).

Current financial donations from the corporate sector constitute 5.4 percent of all donations (Pifer 1987, p. 120). This amount hardly indicates a takeover as a major provider of social services. How far the corporate sector will go in accepting some responsibility to deal with social problems remains to be seen. A question in the late 1980s is whether the corporate sector will continue to donate as it is currently doing.

> *Chief executive officers say the harsh business climate— including 'bottom-line' pressures, changes in ownership, and a 'lean and mean' approach to management—is a threat to company giving* (McMillen 1988, p. A37).

While current CEOs are committed to personal as well as corporate giving, an educator reports that the next generation of executives is much more worried about the business environment placing constraints on charitable giving. What is more, they personally are less likely to be motivated to be active in charitable causes (McMillen 1988, A37–A38).

Some people may expect the corporate sector to take more responsibility for social issues, but the major function of business is to make a profit. Other people think government is responsible for the general welfare of society.

Government Sector

Government in recent years has reduced its financial support of the independent sector. Yet there is a fear that people will reduce their contributions, and people are giving less (see earlier discussion in the section about financial data). What is more difficult to determine is why people are not as concerned about the independent sector as they have been, and what affects their philanthropic and voluntary actions. The question of concern is appropriate to all citizens, but especially to students, because it is youth who are seen as the most unwilling to participate.

Support for the Independent Sector

The Robinson Humanitarian Award recipients do not see their peers as selfish, but rather as people who do not know how to get involved personally in service activities in the independent (or nonprofit) sector (Newman 1987). Researchers have collected information about who college students feel should provide services for society. The results of that research present a different picture than the one the Robinson Humanitarian Award recipients provide.

In 1985, 60.5 percent of students supported national health insurance, and 73.3 percent wanted increased taxation of the wealthy. These percentages have remained fairly constant during the last 10 to 15 years. More recently, however, 78 percent support government intervention to control environmental pollution; 62.4 percent want government to increased consumer protection; and 71.7 percent want government to encourage energy conservation. Overall, 60 to 80 percent of today's freshmen are in favor of increased government regulation (Astin et al. 1987, pp. 19–21).

A study completed in 1988 found that 90 percent of college-age people agree it is the government's responsibility to take care of those who can not take care of themselves; 81 percent believe government should guarantee food and shelter for all; and 73 percent disagree that government is spending too much to help the poor (Hodgkinson and Weitzman 1988, pp. 57–58).

The answers adults give to questions about who should provide services also are indicative of the trend of expecting government to provide for the needs of society. For example:

- When asked if government should play a major role in the support of health care for all Americans, environmental protection, economic development, adequate employment opportunities, basic research, and helping Americans compete in the world market place, between 55 percent and 73 percent answered "yes."
- Eighty-three percent think fostering civil rights is best done by government, and 60 percent of those support legislative action by the federal government.
- In the case of the environment, care for the poor, highway construction, college and university education, elementary and secondary education, and mass transit, 80 percent and more of respondents feel that local, state, and federal governments are best able and should provide the support for these activities and operations (Opinion Roundup 1982, pp. 29–30).

Studies completed in 1984 and 1988 asked the same three questions but got different results.

- When asked whether government has a responsibility to take care of people who cannot take care of themselves,

77 percent agreed in 1984. In 1988, 81 percent agreed.
- In 1984 two-thirds of respondents thought government should guarantee that all citizens had enough to eat and a place to live; in 1988 that percent had increased to 70.
- In 1984, 66 percent did not feel that government was spending too much to assist the poor. In 1988, 67 percent did not think so (Hodgkinson and Weitzman 1988, pp. 57–58; and Yankelovich et al. 1986, p. 47).

It seems the decade of the 1980s may be thought of as a time when American's expectation of government solving social problems increased.

Results of research by Austin et al. (1987) and Hodgkinson and Weitzman (1988) indicate that college students see government as the major provider of services to society. Opinion Roundup (1982), Yankelovich et al. (1986), and Hodgkinson and Weitzman (1988) reach similar conclusions for adults in their research.

Perhaps it should be expected that government will provide for society. The results of one study indicate that a majority of college graduates, 78 percent, do not believe independent sector organizations will be able to solve major social problems (Opinion Roundup 1982, p. 29). And while 82 percent of college-age people believe that charities are important to society, only 48 percent think they spend their money wisely. But 73 percent believe charities are more needed now than five years ago, and 55 percent believe charities are more effective than they were five years ago (Hodgkinson and Weitzman 1988, pp. 58–62).

College-aged students see a need for independent sector agencies, but question whether they will be able to solve the problems that need addressing. Depending on the sources of future funding, they may be correct in their assumption.

Factors Affecting Volunteering
The changing pattern of support of the independent sector is a reflection of the overall changing social and economic conditions of the last 25 years. After World War II and through the better part of the 1960s, most people enjoyed economic security and a fairly stable political environment.

Concerns of those outside the mainstream
Those who were not in the mainstream to receive the social and economic benefits mobilized. Minorities, including both

gender and color, white ethnic groups, and college students all moved into the political arena seeking recognition and the same benefits the majority received (Riesman 1976, p. 21).

The women's movement of the late 1960s and early 1970s saw a reversal of pluralism with women and other minority groups arguing that "bureaucratic social service organizations were exploiting volunteer workers in the name of citizenship" (Reichlin 1982, p. 26).

Great Society efforts

As previously under-recognized groups gained social and economic opportunities, concern for the welfare of society drew attention. The independent sector was expected to provide increased services to address social ills, but it could not do so. The result was increased government support under Great Society legislation. This was an attempt by government to deal with the most difficult social, environmental, and economic problems. The result was the expenditure of huge sums of money that had a direct and traumatic impact on government as well as the private organizations (Pifer 1984, p. 16).

However, the Great Society did not solve social problems and people became disenchanted with it. A new conservativism grew up. One that gave people a feeling of being in positions to serve themselves with less concern for others and a lack of support for government intervention.

Effect on society

The loss of civic concern and involvement can be traced in part to what has just been described. Society has become individualistic, with people focused on their own concerns and working for what they believe are their ideals—regardless of what others are doing. In the case of students, some of the factors which affect them (and may cause them to be less responsive to the needs of others) might be traced to the conditions in which they grew up and which have made an impact on their lives (see chap. 2).

Nonetheless, while the donation of time and money has not increased at the rate of the GNP or personal income, and while both economic and social conditions place many people under greater stress than previous generations have experienced, civic-minded individuals continue to see needs within society and give their time and effort for the welfare of others.

However, the Great Society did not solve social problems and people became disenchanted with it. A new conservatism grew up.

Volunteering

The voluntary activities of U.S. individuals are extensive. One study shows that some 89 million Americans contributed unpaid service to voluntary organizations worth an estimated $110 billion (Pifer 1987, p. 120). While the amount of money may be thought significant, a study completed in 1984 found that just 47 percent of respondents volunteered.

The percent who volunteered dropped even further four years later to 45 percent. These studies confirm the results of previous research; less than half of those who might volunteer do so (Hodgkinson and Weitzman 1988). They also confirm that "giving increases among those who are involved as volunteers, and giving generally increases as the amount of volunteer time increases" (Yankelovich et al. 1986, p. 27).

Of respondents who did not volunteer in 1984, 42 percent gave either less than $100 or nothing, while only 23 percent of those who volunteered gave less than $100 or nothing (Yankelovich et al. 1986). In 1988, research showed that contributions from households where no one volunteered averaged $489.00 (1.3 percent of household income).

The average contribution from households in which volunteers resided was $1,021.00 (2.4 percent of household income) (Hodgkinson and Weitzman 1988, p. 1).

Those studies confirm that fewer people are serving as volunteers. In addition, as a general rule those who do not volunteer do not contribute as much financially as volunteers often do. At the same time, when researchers ask if people are giving what they can to charity financially, 81 percent think they are. And when asked if every person should volunteer to assist others less well off, 78 percent think they should (Yankelovich et al. 1986).

Although four years later those figures had dropped to 75 and 74 percent respectively (Hodgkinson and Weitzman 1988, p. 63), it seems that people think that everyone should be involved in civic matters for the welfare of society, but that less than half are doing so.

In an 1984 study, among respondents who indicated they were very active in community affairs, 72 percent volunteered while only 30 percent of those not active did so (Yankelovich et al 1986, p. 27). Four years later, a similar inquiry on community involvement, levels of contribution, and volunteering found that just 19 percent of those not active in their communities reported household contributions and volunteering while 72 percent of the respondents who were involved both contributed and volunteered (Hodgkinson and Weitzman 1988, p. 53).

There is a clear relationship with the level of community involvement and contribution of volunteer time (Yankelovich et al. 1986, p. 27).

The relationship between community involvement and volunteering may deserve consideration when discussing the youth of today who are seen as isolated from being participatory members of a community. The results of studies by Yankelovich et al. and Hodgkinson and Weitzman reveal that volunteering is more likely to be done by people who are involved in their communities. But researchers, including Boyer and Newman, have determined that students are not active in their college communities.

In 1988, 73 percent of college-age students believed one should contribute to charity, and 72 percent believed they should volunteer to help others. But 46 percent of the group did not contribute, and 58 percent did not volunteer (Hodgkinson and Weitzman 1988, pp. 63–64).

College students are enrolled at institutions that could provide an environment that would offset the effects of changing economic and social conditions. Educational reformers are expressing need to involve students in civic participation. Education is being called upon to create service programs.

Yet others have been concerned for a number of years. Actions to get youth involved have been proposed for over two decades. Some of those proposals have been in the form of federal legislation.

CALL FOR A NATIONAL SERVICE PROGRAM

National service can be defined in many ways. As a general term, it refers to a period of service given by the individual to the nation or community. National service embodies two complementary ideas: one, that some service to the larger society is part of individual citizenship responsibility; and two, that society should be structured in ways which provide citizens with opportunities to make meaningful contributions (Sherraden and Eberly 1982, p. 3).

National Service: A Good Idea

National service which involves people of all races and economic backgrounds could integrate society and do much to eliminate the inequities which exist (Committee for the Study of National Service 1979). It could encourage social participation to foster aspects of human behavior not adequately enhanced by attending college or holding a job. It is a way to achieve specific social needs and national goals that present institutions are unable to reach (Landrum 1979).

Currently, too many people have little concern for others, fail to understand our shared heritage, and do not wish to deal with problems or develop answers. National service for youth could provide a partial solution to these concerns (Levine 1980). It also might be a way to cultivate in youth a sense of citizenship and a feeling of individual responsibility and giving for the sake of the larger community.

It may have the effect, also, of building understanding, tolerance, maturity, and other traits essential for effective performance in business, government, or other activities later in life (Robb 1985, p. 5).

In writing about students, educator Ernest Boyer (1986) said that many are unconnected and isolated from the world around them. With few exceptions, they lack any sense of being needed, have no deep commitments, and find few opportunities to give meaning to their lives. To combat these characteristics Boyer suggests that students complete a term of service.

Another researcher suggested that national service opportunities, full and part-time, paid and unpaid, would provide manpower to change a variety of social problems that now languish from lack of attention. National service would draw college students into the mainstream of society and break

---

them out of the isolation caused by educational institution-
alization. Contemporary youth would become active members
of society (Hogan 1981, pp. 99–102).

Essential Elements of a Service Program
Accepting the need for service programming is one thing.
Guidelines for its creation also are necessary. Robb offers five:

1. The program should mean minimal interruption of people's careers.
2. The emphasis should be on incentives.
3. Youth service should involve a range of options.
4. Fulfillment of the service obligation ought to bring educational benefits.
5. Youth service should not be, at least primarily, an employment program (Robb 1985, p. 5).

To attract youth there should be incentives including tuition
support, educational credit, practical experiences, preferential
college admissions and employment, and in-service education. Service should be something students look forward to
being a part of and participate in positively (Levine 1980,
pp. 137–38).

Students now participate in 12 to 16, and more, years of
formal classroom education followed by four or five decades
of work. Currently there are no large-scale programs offering
the opportunity for full-time service, except the military. But
if a million or more young people who come of age enter
one or two years of full-time service they "would be better
educated and better prepared as workers and citizens" (Committee for the Study of National Service 1979, p. 9).

National service is not a new idea, but the seriousness with
which a number of legislators, educators, commissioners, and
government officials have addressed the topic in the last 20
years make it obvious that there is more than passing interest
in the possibility of required inscription of all youth. The
Committee for the Study of National Service made the following recommendations:

> All young people should be challenged to serve full time for
> one or more years in meeting the needs of the nation and
> the world community. . . . A system for National Service
> should be established to provide opportunities so that at least
> a year of such service after leaving secondary or higher edu-

cation can become a common expectation of young people. . . .

National Service should be organized so as to enable young people to help meet the real economic, social, and educational needs of the nation . . . All present government programs of full-time civilian service . . . should be included among the options in the new system of National Service (1979, pp. 2–3).

Service programs should be open to any young person, aged 16 and older. The military also should be included in recognized national service programming. And people who serve in either non-military or military service should be entitled to the same benefits. In addition, local boards should assist youth in deciding how to best serve the nation. This could be done by creating local service councils to which all youth would go for help in planning.

Ultimately, a national service system would need to be established by Congress and funded through taxes. But leadership for such a program should come from the private sector (Committee for the Study of National Service 1979, pp. 5–6).

The Coalition for National Service lists 10 reasons for creating a national service program (1988). Its "Action Agenda" focused on the growing opportunities, need for more volunteers, and the increasing support for college students to volunteer. It also calls for the establishment of a National Youth Service and a National Youth Service Foundation.

To see the service plan carried out, the Coalition proposes several pilot projects such as creating a clearinghouse of activities, evaluating service needs in communities, and surveying what youths do for voluntary activities. It seeks to expand current opportunities, link opportunities together, garner public support, and ensure that ultimately the entire nation is involved (Coalition for National Service 1988, pp. 3–24).

Congressional Efforts to Create National Service Programs

In 1966 a proposal was made to create a foundation to underwrite a civilian national service corps. The military draft still existed and every male had to register. It was conceived that when registering, young men would indicate a preference for either military or nonmilitary service, and would enter one or the other.

Another plan was meant to address a concern about the number of young men who avoided service through educational deferments. The sponsor thought that a service corps would be educational and would make use of the talented students avoiding military service.

A third Congressional proposal called for requiring all young men at age 18 to attend a three-month orientation and then select either military on nonmilitary service.

A fourth plan called for the creation of a multi-tier program ultimately involving 200,000 volunteers; most would enter existing programs in the United States.

While none of the plans became realities, they led the way for future proposals (Eberly and Sherraden 1982b). In 1969 Senator Mark Hatfield proposed the creation of the Youth Power Act. His bill was meant to create enough opportunities so that all youth could serve and learn. It was not meant to replace, but rather to supplement and increase the service and learning opportunities available to young people.

Efforts in the 1970s

In 1970 a congressman introduced a bill in the House titled "The National Service Act of 1970." The bill would have created a civilian service system similar to the military service system, but services would have provided for the nation's social welfare.

In 1979 another bill, "The National Service Act," was meant to end the Military Service Act and replace it with a civilian service program. In 1979 Representative John Cavanaugh introduced the Public Service System Act, a bill that incorporated several unique features. None, however, survived the legislative process.

- Young people would be required to enter civilian service.
- All civilian service would be performed in federal agencies.
- Within four and one-half years of enactment, most federal agencies would have to set aside five percent of their positions for individuals entering civilian service (Eberly and Sherraden 1982b).

During the 1980s a number of hearings regarding the support of volunteer activities were held. On April 22, 1982, for example, 14 representatives of business, industry, fraternal orders, and education testified before a subcommittee of the

United States Senate. The hearings focused on who should support civic activities that benefit society.

Background information
During the 20 years preceding the 1980s, federal expenditures increased from $20 billion to $300 billion for social programs. The result of the massive increase in spending was an equally massive increase in the federal deficit. This growth of federal support had conditioned people to expect government to take the major responsibility for solving any and all social problems, both current and future, that society may confront (U.S. Congress. Senate. Hearing 1982).

Reagan Administration viewpoint. From the perspective of the Reagan administration, it was time that individuals and businesses took back the major responsibility for funding and providing needed services. It was time for government support to be reduced. Individuals and private organizations needed encouragement to become more involved in helping those with special needs (U.S. Congress. Senate. Hearing 1982).

Those speaking on behalf of President Reagan emphasized that his call for more private initiatives and a revival of volunteerism was made because such actions were "right in their own regard," and not to offset federal budget cuts. But those who testified indicated that the independent and corporate sectors could not replace the contribution that government made for the welfare of society.

Voluntary National Youth Service Act and Select Commission on National Service Opportunities Act
In 1985 two bills were introduced dealing with the volunteer service of youth in the United States. House Bill 1326 was proposed to establish a commission to examine issues related to national service. The commission's focus was the need for such a service, and an assessment of the current opportunities and activities which existed for youth to serve society (Voluntary National Youth Service Act and the Select Commission on National Service Opportunities Act of 1985, 1985, pp. 13–24).

House Bill 888, proposed by Leon Panetta (R-Calif.), called for the creation of a national service corps. The bill's provisions included:

- serving in both traditional and nontraditional arenas where voluntary efforts had historically been applied
- job training aimed at reducing youth unemployment
- paying participants in the range of 80 to 160 percent of the current minimum wage, depending on responsibilities
- requiring service for a year, although a person could volunteer for two years
- requiring volunteers to be between 17 and 24, and high school graduates.

The bill also called for the service corps to be funded with matching grants. It also called for federal dollars to be joined with state and/or local dollars to create the program.

Viewpoints expressed at hearings. Those who testified in favor of the bill expressed concern over the decreasing number of youth who were involved in civic service. In 1985 there were fewer than 2,500 people age 26 and younger involved in VISTA and the Peace Corps. Advocates said that a national service program was needed because the free enterprise system had failed to meet the needs of people in the United States.

Reformers maintained that while material needs were being met, the United States had some serious shortcomings. These included: a lack of quality education for youth; few ways to protect people from pollution or to preserve the natural surroundings of the nation. Other shortcomings listed were a failure to eliminate illiteracy, to provide compassion or companionship for millions of Americans living alone or in institutions, and to nurture and stimulate Americans to be active citizens.

Overall, advocates observed at hearings, there was a failure to engage young Americans to help meet these and other needs (The Voluntary National Youth Service Act and the Select Commission on National Service Opportunities Act of 1985).

Support for the bill. The Council for the Advancement of Citizenship, the Red Cross, the Catholic Church, the presidents of several colleges and universities, and other prominent individuals all supported the passage and funding of Panetta's National Service Bill.

Hearings were concluded in 1985, and the bill was referred to the Subcommittee on Education and Labor. It resurfaced as part of the Higher Education Amendments Act of 1986 which was carried over to 1987, and then referred to a subcommittee on Labor and Human Resources.

Bills proposed by the 100th Congress
When the 100th Congress convened in 1987 several new bills were introduced to create a national service program.

In the Senate, the Voluntary National Service and the Education Demonstration Acts supported state education authorities in operating service programs and administering a GI-type program for people who completed two years of civilian or military service. The bill proposed the authorization of $30 million a year for five years to pay for programs.

Another Senate bill wanted to amend the Higher Education Act of 1965 by allowing partial cancellation of loans for full-time service with a tax exempt agency.

A House bill was the first to propose eliminating the federal financial aid program components of loans and grants and instituting a requirement that those seeking financial aid had to spend time in either military or civilian service.

Representative Panetta reintroduced his National Youth Service Act bill. Another House bill sought to create a national conservation corps, similar to one passed in 1984 but vetoed by President Reagan.

Yet another House bill called for a Commission on National Service Opportunities to create a program and plan to study voluntary opportunities in the area of national service. (National Service Secretariat 1987, pp. 1, 4).

In 1988 in the House, the American Conservation Corps bill (HR 18) and the Voluntary National Youth Service bill (HR 460) cleared two committees. However, Congress adjourned before either went to a full vote (National Service Secretariat 1988b, pp. 1–2).

Bills proposed by the 101st Congress
The 101st Congress saw over 20 bills presented to it in 1989. Some proposals are viewed as controversial because they included a provision requiring service for students in return for financial aid.

Nunn-McCurdy bill. None of the bills was more controversial than the Citizenship and National Service Act bill proposed by Senator Sam Nunn and Representative David McCurdy (Wilson 1989a, p. A20). (For the rationale behind the Nunn-McCurdy legislation, see Moskos 1988.)

Supporters for tying federal financial aid to service included the Democratic Leadership Council, the United States Junior Chamber of Commerce and the College Democrats of America. However, a number of House and Senate members as well as members of the education community did not support the link (Kuntz 1989, p. 647; Wilson 1989a, pp. A20–A21).

In hearings held to discuss the Nunn-McCurdy bill, the American Council on Education and 11 other higher education groups endorsed the testimony for a national service bill, but opposed the phase-out aspect regarding financial aid (Newsletter of the American Council on Education 1989b, pp. 1–2). According to the bill, Pell Grants, Supplemental Opportunity Grants, and State Student Incentive Grants would be phased out. In addition, a period of service would be a requirement to receive loans.

Several senators thought that proven financial aid programs should not be replaced but supplemented (Newsletter of the American Council on Education 1989a). The bill's authors estimated the program would draw about 700,000 volunteers a year, while the Federal aid programs serve about two million first year students annually (Ford 1989).

Arguments pro and con. Those who favored tying financial aid to service argued that current aid programs are not meeting their purposes, there is a great deal of default on educational loans, and the budget deficit is a negative factor for increasing the aid funding (Wilson 1989a, p. A21).

Opponents expressed several concerns including the question of whether tying financial aid to service might create even more barriers for poor and minority students, the ones for whom financial aid is meant to provide a means to a college education. It also could permit wealthy students to enroll without having to serve (Wilson 1989b, p. A19).

Financial incentives for service. All volunteers would be the recipients of entitlement vouchers for $10,000 to $12,000 for each year served to be used for education or a down payment on a house. No one would have to demonstrate financial need as is now required in the federally funded financial aid programs. It is thought that for those students needing financial aid the most, college attendance could well be something that would not take place if they had to wait two years before enrolling, and in giving grants for the amounts proposed, students might have to either borrow to attend a college of choice, or select one that was less expensive (Ford 1989, P. A40; and Wilson 1989b, p. A19 & A24).

Cost as an issue. The cost of implementing the Nunn-McCurdy proposal was also an issue. While proponents of the bill expected it to cost $5 billion more annually than current financial aid programs, the American Council on Education estimated that when it was participated in fully, costs could rise as much as $50 billion more, not the $13 billion estimated by the authors of the bill (Newsletter of the American Council on Education 1989a, p. 4).

[Tying financial aid to service] could permit wealthy students to enroll without having to serve.

Student views. While a majority of college officials disapproved of Senator Nunn's proposed legislation, some students considered it long overdue. Some saw it as a way to correct a system which appears to grant aid to those who do not deserve it. Others saw service as a way for those who get financial aid to pay society back for that money.

While it is safe to say that most students had not heard of the proposal, those who knew about it said that the proposal sounds attractive.

Many said they would have participated if such a program had been in place before they enrolled in their colleges and universities (Wilson 1989b, p. A19).

But students, like college and university officials, are concerned that such a program of voluntary service would become a program of the poor because the poor would be forced to serve. They support the service concept, but they oppose the changes to the existing financial aid programs. Students also oppose mandatory service requirements. They recommend a system of incentives such as educational stipends, returning work-study programs to their original intent of providing experiential learning opportunities through community service, and offering students who volunteer after college some type of loan forgiveness (Myers 1989, p. A22).

Students are also concerned that service opportunities would be predominantly low-skill jobs. And they are concerned that such a service program, while offering students the chance to do something for society while earning money for college, would not teach youth that volunteering should be done throughout their lifetimes. They support a volunteer program in which participation would be for all four years of college, not for one or two years preceding matriculation (Wilson 1989b, p. A24).

Other bills

In 1989, in addition to the Nunn-McCurdy bill, several others were also proposed.

- Representative Leon Panetta reintroduced his bills to establish a Youth Service Corps and an American Conservation Corps.

He had some 85 co-sponsors and a Senate version sponsored by Senator Christopher Dodd. Panetta's proposals were meant to provide matching grants to states and local programs to have young people, aged 16 through 25, serve society by working on community service or conservation projects. This would help them gain experience, further education, and a sense of worth. Panetta estimated his bills would cost $152.4 million the first year.

- Senator Barbara Mikulski introduced the National Community Service Act.

Its unique feature was the provision that students could fulfill their service obligation on weekends. Participants would receive a payment of $3,000 for education and/or a down payment on a home. Participation would be for three to six years, with an initial group of 50,000 participants beginning in 1991 at a cost of $250 million.

- Senator Pell reintroduced legislation similar to that he introduced two years ago to authorize state higher education agencies to run service programs.

He proposed that youth serve two years in either community or military service. For their service, participants would receive $250 per month and tuition for 18 months, but not more than $7,200 annually, and a maximum of $14,400. Pell estimated that a five-year demonstration program to test his proposal would cost $35 million (Griffith 1989).

Other bills were also introduced. These included: a House bill similar to that of Nunn-McCurdy but without the requirement of national service for college financial aid. Another House bill called for creating a program to grant a three-year college scholarship for post-graduate service in the Peace Corps.

Senate bills would permit college students to have a partial write-off of student loans for the performance of community service (National Service Secretariat 1989, pp. 1–2).

Compromise bill of 1989

A compromise bill, S.1430, was introduced in the summer of 1989 by eight Democratic Senators who all had introduced their own service bills earlier. They included, Christopher Dodd, Bob Graham, Edward Kennedy, Barbara Mikulski, Daniel Moynihan, Sam Nunn, Claiborne Pell, and Jim Robb.

The bill's provisions included:

1. The partial forgiveness of college loans for serving full time.
2. Changing how the Work-Study program is funded to increase the federal contribution when the jobs are community service, but reducing it for other types of jobs.
3. A request for $300 million in funding, with $100 million to create a Youth Service Corps and demonstration programs in a few states. Demonstration programs included trying ways to connect financial aid to service, creating a National Trust, and emphasizing that community service programs should be educational in their purpose (Stroud 1989, p. 4). A set-aside of 50 percent for community service in the State Student Incentive Grant Program would be created if funding exceeded $75 million.
4. Expanding the VISTA program and programs for older volunteers. Volunteers, aged 15 to 25, would be paid up to $7,500 a year and $5,200 a year in educational benefits.
5. The demonstration project would pay a stipend of up to $7,000 a year and provide volunteers with $8,500 a year for either housing or educational benefits for up to two years of full-time service. Those who chose to serve part time could earn up to $3,000 a year for three to six years of service (DeLoughry 1989, p. A16; Newsletter of the American Council on Education 1989c, pp. 1–2).

How the bill fared. In March 1990 "the Senate passed the National and Community Service Act of 1990 (S. 1430) by a vote of 78 to 19" (National Service Secretariat 1990, p. 1). The bill calls for spending $125 million through September 1991 for national service projects, community service projects, funding of existing programs, and the creation of demonstration programs.

The idea of providing participants a stipend or vouchers was passed, but not without controversy. The bill then moved to the House, where it died in committee.

It seems that in Congress the Democrats are taking a lead in trying to create a national service program. The Republicans, however, are not without their own plan. Their proposal is centered on that of President Bush.

President Bush's Volunteer Program

President Bush presented his plan, *Youth Engaged in Service* or *YES*, in 1989. His plan has at its heart a public/private foundation known as the *Thousand Points of Light Initiative*. The program is meant to take successful service projects and spread them throughout the country. Its provisions include:

- preparing students to serve as leaders
- establishing forums where students can share information about service
- awarding those who are outstanding (DeLoughry and Myers 1989, pp. A14, A19).

President Bush's volunteer service program differs in three ways from the proposals on Capital Hill, according to C. Gregg Petersmeyer, deputy assistant to the President and director of the Office of National Service.

1. It takes into consideration all the people of the nation as volunteers, not just students, or students of one age group.
2. It offers no financial incentives to participate. Instead, it expects that service will not be a federally mandated activity, but a national movement.
3. It sees service as a lifelong undertaking.

Unlike the bills beings sponsored with rewards for serving two or three years, the *Thousand Points of Light Initiative* is meant to expose individuals to the success that can be achieved by volunteers early in their lives. Then they will participate and receive satisfaction through service for the rest of their lives (Ivory 1989, p. 6).

President Bush asked Congress to provide $25 million to begin the program. This request is a quarter of what he proposed during his campaign for the Presidency. While the request asks for the $25 million annually for four years, advocates see it as far less than is necessary to create any type of volunteer program (DeLoughery and Myers 1989, pp. A14, A19).

Reaction to the President's Proposal
The proposal has met with mixed reactions from both campus people and legislators. Some support it, while others see it as too little and lacking the necessary funding to make the idea come to fruition.

Critics think the proposal will have little impact on higher education. Those in higher education see the concept as positive, but think that the proposal to create demonstration projects is one they already have done through their networking (DeLoughry and Myers 1989, pp. A14, A19).

Summary. National service might well be one of the major topics of the early 1990s. During the 1980s, interest in creating a national service program has generated a number of proposals. At the same time, a number of federal, state, and local agencies and organizations are providing service opportunities. And while these are often not considered "national" in scope, taken together they are a sort of patchwork national service blanket.

Actions to Create Local Service Programs
In the 20th century, the Civilian Conservation Corps, the Peace Corps, the Job Corps, Volunteers in Service to America, and a variety of youth employment programs have attempted to meet social needs and involve massive numbers of youths on a national level.

In each case, people participate and society benefits from the services provided. In almost every case, the organization was created in response to a national or world need. It then disappears when social and/or economic conditions change, or only involves a few thousand individuals. Nonetheless, this does not mean that such service programs are not useful or have not worked at local levels (Eberly and Sherraden 1982a).

Model programs
Program for Local Service. In Seattle, a model program, Program for Local Service (PLS), was created in 1973-74. The program called for young people to gain work experience in a voluntary community position for a year. While concern was expressed that few youth would volunteer, the results proved that concern unfounded. Though the program was not obligatory, hundreds of youth from diverse socio-economic backgrounds participated, working in over 1,000 positions. The project was federally funded and evaluated as highly successful (Eberly 1984; Eberly and Sherraden 1982a).

> *The two most dramatic findings relate to the two major reasons given by young people for joining PLS: namely, contributing to the community and gaining work experience. The sponsoring agencies estimated the work done by PLS Volunteers to be worth $2,150,000, double the $1,086,000 federal grant which funded the program. And the unemployment rate among persons in PLS fell from 70 percent at the time of application to 18 percent six months after leaving PLS* (Eberly and Sherraden 1982a, p. 50).

Youth Community Service (YCS). This project was located in Syracuse, N.Y., from 1978 to 1980.

> *In just under two years the YCS project developed 2,456 positions. If the same proportion of positions were developed nationally, there would be some 1,100,000* (Eberly and Sherraden 1982a, p. 50).

Additional youth projects
In 1984 there were 10 separate actions taken to sponsor, and/or require, youth to participate in some type of service activity. Attempts to create service corps on the state or local level occurred in California, New York, Oregon, Virginia, Minnesota, and in Georgia. On a national level, the National Association of Secondary School Principals (NASSP) made grants to 11 schools to implement the service recommendations of Ernest Boyer (Eberly 1985).

In addition to state, local, and other efforts to create programs to increase student volunteerism, advocates of student volunteerism sought continued government support. For instance, in Virginia, the governor called for a nationwide conference to ". . . examine youth service in relationship to school dropouts and youth unemployment." In New York, the governor ". . . asked the legislature to appropriate $7 million to begin a statewide youth service corps." In Kentucky, the ". . . Committee on Academic Excellence is expected to recommend that all high school students be required to participate in service-learning programs" (Eberly 1985, pp. 87–88).

In 1987, two Boston colleges were the first to train students to participate in the National Literacy Corps. Senator Kennedy planned to introduce legislation to expand the program to 1,000 colleges and universities. In 1988, there were statewide service program initiatives in Minnesota, Pennsylvania, California, Iowa, and Massachusetts.

Incentives are part of most of the proposed programs. In Minnesota, college students who commit 15 hours per week will be awarded $1,500 scholarships at specified campuses. The proposed program in Massachusetts will offer tuition vouchers to all youth who volunteer for one or two years. In California the Human Corps bill was approved; it is meant to put pressure on college students to volunteer 30 hours of civic service during an academic year. The law requires all public colleges to find community service opportunities for their students (Blumenstyk 1989, p. A20; Neiman 1988, p. 3).

Colleges and universities also have begun to organize. The presidents of Stanford, Georgetown, and Brown universities and the Education Commission of the States formed the Campus Compact in 1985. Its purpose is

> to create a campus environment in which volunteer activity becomes an integral part of the undergraduate experience—by appointing paid program directors, offering service fellowships, and providing recognition for student volunteers. The Compact's executive office (at Brown) works with federal, state, and local governments to establish programs promoting campus service (Theus 1988, pp. 31–32).

The Campus Compact produces a newsletter, gives the Robinson Humanitarian Achievement Awards, assists member institutions to create programs, and is working to involve students in national volunteer programs (Theus 1988, p. 32).

While actions of the Campus Compact are the type educational reformers such as Boyer, Newman, and others are calling for higher education to take, at question is whether students will volunteer in significant numbers.

Youth Support for National Service

Will youth participate in a national service program? A 1979 Gallup study found that 71 percent of teenagers (13 to 18 years old) and 77 percent of young adults (18 to 24 years old) favored a program of voluntary national service. When the question of mandatory service was raised, 42 percent of young adults favored inscription. Other studies also found teenagers and young adults favoring some type of service program (Hedin 1982, chap. 14).

Gallup studies have found that seven of eight adults support a program of community service for students.

In 1984 the results of a Gallup survey indicated that 65 percent of American adults favored a one-year compulsory national service program (with educational benefits), with 58 percent of young people (aged 18–24), favoring the same (Dolan 1986, p. 10).

In 1988 a Gallup Poll reported that voluntary national service was favored by 89 percent of the public; 11 percent opposed it; and 6 percent had no opinion.

That is the highest level of support achieved for either voluntary or mandatory national service since Gallup began polling on the question in 1969 (National Service Secretariat 1988a, p. 2).

Support for voluntary national service is strong among 18 to 24 year olds, those who would serve in such a program. Eighty-seven percent favor the creation of a service program. These results caused Donald J. Eberly, executive director of the National Service Secretariat, to challenge individuals who label young people the "Me" generation.

Young people are not lacking in a desire to serve as much as our country is failing to give them opportunities to serve. . . . I challenge the next President to create a voluntary national service corps that asks young people to serve on the frontiers of human need (National Service Secretariat 1988b, p. 2).

Some students "favored a mandatory community-service requirement for all college students" (Collison 1989a, p. A34). Others think that alternative proposals are needed. One student indicated that altering the work-study program to include more funding for community service could accomplish much of what proposed legislation would do. Other students see the proposals undermining the growing number of college students who choose to volunteer on their own, and distorting the notion of volunteerism by requiring them to serve (Collison 1989a, p. A34).

National Service: Impact on Higher Education

Youth currently have the option to work, join the military, attend college, or be unemployed. If a youth service program existed which attracted one to two million people, 18 to 24 years old, what impact would it have on higher education? It is estimated that, in addition to any drop in the number of 18 to 24 year olds who might attend college, an additional 230,000 would not enroll if a national service program existed. At the same time, if such a program offered educational vouchers, the number of older students who would enter college might increase (but their attendance might be primarily as part-time students). Consequently, the creation of a national service program is seen as something that will decrease the enrollment of traditional-aged students (Ramsay 1982).

Elements of national service proposals

National service proposals include the voluntary or mandatory involvement of between 200,000 and a million or more youth in an initial year with a projected increase in the numbers in successive years (Landrum 1979, pp. 97–103).

Funding. To begin and sustain a national youth service program of the size proposed would require a significant amount of money. The costs could be met by raising new money or by redirecting current funds. In redirecting funds, the question is from which programs could money be taken. One under consideration is higher education (Landrum 1979, pp. 120–27).

A national service program would be educational, would take all youth into service, and would provide the opportunities for further education through either some sort of grant or other means. The total cost is projected to be between $500 million and $8 billion annually (proposals such as the one made by Nunn and McCurdy are expected to cost a great deal more).

Federal funding of higher education includes monies meant for equality of opportunity. In 1977, money for financial assistance of disadvantaged students totaled $7.4 billion. During the 1986-1987 academic year students received $20.5 billion in financial aid in the form of loans, grants, and through federal employment programs. In 1989 an unduplicated 6.5 million students received financial aid. Yet Nunn-McCurdy and similar proposals linking financial aid to service would dismantle such programs while expecting from half a million to a million young people to participate (Evangelauf 1987b; Newman 1989).

A national service program linking financial aid to service also is conceived of as a way to provide equal opportunity. Monies now designated for financial aid awards would be redirected to service programs involving youth. In addition, the funding of federal education, employment, or welfare assistance could be made contingent on previous service to society.

Redirecting funds from the military, tax revenues, social and welfare services, and higher education could fund a national service program. Some people ask if doing so would increase inflation. However the idea of increased inflation is made moot if people see the creation of such programming as an investment rather than an additional layer of federal bureaucracy. It also is rendered moot if people take into consideration the fact that taking part in service programs could enhance participants' productive capacities and make them likely to contribute more to the gross national product.

In other words, if those in national service contribute tangible assets that more than offset the expense involved, the national economy stands to benefit in the long run (Landrum 1979, pp. 126–127)

Effect of proposals on disadvantaged
Productivity and employability often are seen as outcomes of higher education. Financial aid programs were created to provide equal access to a college education. Access is meant for the disadvantaged and more students can enter a college or university with financial aid.

What impact changing the current financial aid programs might have is an important question to consider. The question is whether college access for the disadvantaged would increase or decrease by making grants, such as the Pell grant, available only after service is given for a one- or two-year period. Currently, those from the lowest economic bracket are eligible for the most financial aid. Research on the use of the Basic Educational Opportunity Grants (now Pell Grants) indicates that enrollments are 60 percent higher among low-income students, 12 percent higher among middle-income students, and 3 percent higher among upper-income students.

Using the 1979 Pell Grant program as an indicator, if service were a condition of a grant, more than 37 out of 100 low-income students would find providing service to be a practical prerequisite to continuing their education past high school, while only 10 out of every 100 middle-income students and fewer than 3 out of every 100 upper-income students would confront the same requirement (Danzig and Szanton 1986, p. 231).

For [some youth], a service program that ties financial aid to volunteering could detour, if not remove, them from ever entering higher education.

It is estimated that some 40 percent of youth would not consider going to college, even with the grants. For others, a service program that ties financial aid to volunteering could detour, if not remove, them from ever entering higher education. Critics like Thomas H. Kean, president of Drew University, express concern over any bill that would tie financial aid to college funding because "it hits unevenly. If you happen to be rich, you don't worry about it" (Blumenstyk 1989, p. A20).

Educational benefits of youth service
While enrollment figures might change for colleges and universities, the educational benefits of a service program could offset them, depending on the role higher education chooses to take. Students seeking to matriculate in college probably would do so after a period of service just as they would do before serving. But for students not planning to enter college, a period of service might cause them to become more conscious and interested in further education.

A national service program could offer many opportunities to provide part-time and other special educational opportunities while young people served (Ramsay 1982, p. 136). Youth also could be attracted to higher education if they knew they would receive credit for what they learned while in service.

Programs in place to implement proposal
Many programs needed for advancing people and awarding credit are already in place. These include, for instance, the Graduation Equivalency Diploma (GED), evaluation of experiences by the American Council on Education, College Level Examination Program (CLEP) examinations, other standardized tests used for the evaluation of knowledge gained from non-collegiate learning, and evaluation of knowledge gained from life experiences.

College students who would opt to enter a service program could be granted service-learning credit, and other opportunities to recognize formally their accomplishments and increased knowledge (Ramsay 1982).

Assistance in evaluating student's learning experiences could be secured as could help in putting together meaningful educational service-learning or internship programs. The Council on Adult and Experiential Learning (CAEL) has published a number of books, reports, and a Jossey-Bass New Directions series, on a variety of topics dealing with the creation of programs and evaluation of learning that takes place outside the classroom.

CAEL also is active in research to provide quality control in the granting of credit for life experience. The National Society for Internships and Experiential Education (NSIEE) provides colleges and universities a number of services including directories listing internship opportunities for students and professional development opportunities for faculty and staff (Swager 1985, p. 118).

National Service Concept
Will national service solve all the problems its proponents believe it should? Some see national service as only an ideal and not as an operational program. While such a program is supported politically and could be carried out under the Constitution, there is the question of what the operation of such a program would really cost the government, and therefore the taxpayer.

Unquestionably there is enough that needs doing in the United States to put over two million youth to work. But whether such a program would do all that proponents say it would is questionable. For instance, it is unlikely that all participants would go to college; their participation in the program, therefore, would bring them no benefit from college credit or tuition vouchers.

Similarly, it is unlikely that all participants would receive practical job training that would prove useful later. The idea that national service would solve the youth unemployment problem is also questionable. In a one- or two-year commitment, too few positions can be offered to 18 year olds that will translate into post-service career positions.

What alternatives to national youth service are there?

To some extent a national service program is grasping for solutions to a number of social problems which need addressing. In other words, can other ways of addressing the problems be found? More choices need to be developed for youth, along with more ways for them to service society voluntarily. If the goal is getting youth involved, and helping them learn to be active citizens, then perhaps other ways could be created that would do the same thing (Danzig and Szanton 1986).

A growing number of reformers, including members of the Democratic Leadership Council and The Coalition for National Service, believe that voluntary service will be put into the educational structure (Dolan 1986). A number of universities and colleges have accepted the challenge of enhancing students' civic education by creating and emphasizing volunteer service programs of their own. With activities on college and university campuses linked to agencies and organizations working to get students involved in service, the grassroots beginnings of a national service program exist (Swearer 1985, pp. 6-7).

A call for grassroots efforts. National service should not be a federally sponsored make-work project. Rather, efforts should be started at the university, local, and state levels. Efficient coordination should create a rational well-run federal program (Swearer 1985, p. 7). There needs to be

active participation by educational institutions, including the operation of National Service projects. Faculty and staff members who would otherwise be engaged in a teaching role would be challenged to examine community needs and to manage local National Service operations. In the process,

*these educators, some of whom will resist the idea, will dis-
cover it is a learning experience for them as well as the
young people* (Eberly and Sherraden 1982c, pp. 216–217).

However, even those who see education as a proper starting
point for the creation of service programs also believe that
some sort of national service program is needed. While there
are those concerned with the potential of a program that is
run by the federal government, there is also concern over
what type of programs colleges would operate. But it is possible for education to operate programs successfully.

Colleges and universities are in a special position to instill a sense of civic responsibility and, consequently, to shape public policy through the actions of their graduates. The current inactivity on the part of higher education seems to have placed an entire generation outside the realm of society where values and a vision are created that are universally shared.

Education of college students to be citizens should go beyond classroom rhetoric and put the students into participatory situations in their communities to work in anti-poverty, anti-illiteracy, and anti-apartheid programs. There is neither enough classroom teaching about the diversity of social structure and economic status in the United States, nor is there enough encouragement or opportunity for students to become actively involved in providing services to those in need (McMillen 1987, pp. A33–A34).

Needed Curricular Changes

The call by so many people to have students participate in service programming is due partly to the desire to have adolescents enter adulthood with a sense of citizenship and with positive social values (Landrum 1979). Concern over the attitudes of college students in the 1980s is coming from a variety of sources including the reports released about the status of higher education and what should be done to change it.

The report, *To Secure the Blessings of Liberty,* includes discussion about students' diminishing interest in civic responsibility. The report portrays higher education as having a long history of preparing students for civic participation and leadership. The contemporary collegiate experience, however, appears to be one in which career aspirations and personal goals are emphasized by curricula that are laden with vocationalism and lack emphasis on teaching the responsibilities of being a citizen in a democracy (The National Commission on the Role and Future of State Colleges and Universities 1986, p. 10).

Changes in curricula and course requirements also may reflect our increasingly technological society. But neither technology nor student goals should be the reasons "for abandoning requirements that are essential to our students' intellectual and social growth" (Slaughter 1985, p. 43).

Students must learn that it is not enough to be successful as managers, lawyers, or doctors—by making money, winning the big case, or gaining positions of economic power. They must learn that they can make a difference (Levine 1986, p. 6). Consequently, for contemporary youth

> *an education that stresses the ability to think, to evaluate, to understand ethical and social issues is absolutely essential in this complex world we live in. The intellectual and social growth of our students is critically important for the future of our society. . . . The most critical demand is to restore to higher education its original purpose of preparing graduates for a life of involved citizenship. It is a need which arises from the unfolding array of societal issues of enormous complexity and seriousness* (Slaughter 1985, p. 45).

Higher education could do two things to institute change in how contemporary youth enter adulthood; these changes would alter their views of a collegiate education and instill a sense of service to society.

- Change current curricular offerings.
- Make opportunities available for students to experience volunteer activities.

Altering curricular offerings should be done with the idea of increasing students' social motivation and competency. Greater emphasis in social studies classes on the use of the scientific method might increase students' desire to analyze prejudices and see more clearly the oneness of community across the borders of race, religion, and nationality (Rushton 1982, p. 445).

Curricular changes also should include study of the dreams humans have had for society. These should be taught through courses in the behavioral sciences, the arts, and literature. In addition, curricular changes should place an emphasis on personal sacrifice for the welfare of others. Altruism as a human characteristic can be encouraged, even taught, but colleges and universities must be willing to do the instruction by creating curricula to achieve this (Rushton 1982, pp. 442–46).

In addition, civic literacy should be included in college courses. An interested and informed electorate is necessary for the maintenance of our democratic society. Contemporary youths must take up their responsibilities for dealing with the complex, highly technical, and value-laden issues facing them if they are to become members of our society (Futter 1986, p. 47).

But for contemporary youths to be able to participate they must be literate. They must be able to read and write, preferably both English and a foreign language. They must be competent in mathematics, the natural sciences, and technology. And they must know, and understand, the history of U.S. institutions. They also need to know world history, and they need a more sophisticated understanding of the condition of society.

To achieve those goals more than the formal educational setting must be used. Youths need

a place for questioning, for argumentation, for the revival of the texture and . . . the important substantive outcomes of community (Futter 1986, p. 52).

What should opportunities for volunteering provide?

An altered curricula needs to stimulate learning by engaging students in activities. It should provide opportunities for students to gain greater self-esteem. It also should encourage students to take risks. They need to confront the unknown. By introducing students to the unknown, and by having students work with the unknown, the fear of the unknown will diminish as students deal with their fears.

Students need the opportunity to apply theory. They need to apply academic concepts in laboratory settings. Experiential learning can provide laboratory experiences. Students can have direct involvement in basic social institutions through service opportunities and internships. By becoming active participants, students will interact with diverse people. They also will learn how nonprofit organizations operate.

Finally, the most important contribution experiential learning may make in a curricula emphasizing the civic arts would be in the

ability to train students in those process skills which underlie democratic functions—skills related to the individual's participation in groups; and skills such as problem-solving, forms of decision-making, and conflict resolution (MacArthur 1985, p. 10).

To get students involved in the experience of providing services, experiential programming is being called for. But what type of experiential programming is most appropriate? There are several ways that "hands on" experiences in providing assistance to others can be made available and/or recognized.

Service-Learning Education

Service-learning is a form of experiential education meant to integrate working at a public task with educational growth. Service-learning can put college students into situations where they must participate, care, and reach beyond themselves because the lives of other people are affected. It also carries moral considerations because students are dealing with people in real situations.

Results of a study of 4,000 students who participated in 20 programs found that 93 percent said they increased their concern for others. In another study of self-reported feelings from 321 students who participated in 13 service-learning projects, 99 percent gave the same response (Swager 1985, pp. 115–16).

Service-learning also provides a testing ground where theory learned in the classroom can be put to practical application. Students often complain that they fail to see any correlation between their practical experiences and the more theoretical aspects of classroom activities (Swager 1985; Wagner 1987).

When dealing with the idea of community and community problems, students often fail to make a connection between a campus problem and problems of other types in the wider world outside the college campus. Likewise, students who learn skills in practical experiences often fail to apply them to their college work.

In other words, there often is a separation of academic work and practical application. The inability to connect the theoretical with the practical may reduce students' intellectual capacity, making them less thoughtful, and less willing to pose and test research questions.

This separation parallels similar disjunctions between action and reflection or between theory and practice, disjunctions that colleges and universities have a special responsibility to transcend (Wagner 1987, p. 29).

Service-learning provides students the opportunity to explore careers, to do research, and to determine procedures to deal with a variety of problems and situations. Service-learning can also help teach and solidify the skills that the corporate sector wants the people it employs to possess (Swager 1985, p. 117).

Service-learning is a way to educate while involving students in participatory educational experiences. It might be considered a more formal way to structure a volunteer service program into the curriculum.

College Work-Study Program

While the work-study program makes it possible for students to earn money to attend college, it has two other advantages.

It encourages the development of those values students need in our society, and it allows for the opportunity to create public service roles for students both on and off campus (Newman 1985, p. 85).

Newman thinks that work-study program regulations should be rewritten so that colleges and universities are required "to use at least 20 percent of their work-study funds for public service on and off campus." By allocating work-study funds for students to have positions in community service agencies rather than on campus, higher education would provide support for increasing the voluntary participation of students (Danzig and Szanton 1986, p. 182).

Originally, the work-study program was meant to have students perform services in their local communities. However, because employers pay just 20 percent of each dollar paid to the student, college officials have kept most workers on campus. If the 80 percent federal contribution were routed directly to the voluntary agencies rather than through financial aid offices, a much stronger service effort might be guaranteed (Eberly and Sherraden 1982a, p. 46; Newman 1985, p. 199).

Alterations to the college work-study program are a way to involve youth in volunteering. Another way some colleges and universities are getting students involved in activities to increase their civic awareness is to create special programs and/or alter specific courses at their institutions.

Programs at Colleges and Universities

The following examples describe some of the ways higher education is helping students to participate in service activities. The programs described are meant to offer a range of examples, rather than only the largest or best known.

College campus volunteers

Students are active as volunteers on many campuses.
Each year over 1,000 Yale University students work in the community with juvenile offenders, immigrants, and staff of a shelter for homeless people. Princeton University students tutor inner city youth, visit social agencies to see clients, and work with a program offering disadvantaged youngsters the opportunity to interact with nature.

Vanderbilt University students participate in a program which provides medical examinations to rural poor people, conducts health fairs and classes, and works in other health related projects and services. Kent State University students volunteer to help fellow students who are disabled, counsel new students, and work in health and crisis programs (Boyer 1986, pp. 215-216).

Standford University's experience

At Stanford University a fellowship program was created to encourage public service. Alumni provided students assistance to help them consider public sector careers. The law school created a loan forgiveness program so graduates could accept public service positions. Internship programs, and a volunteer center/clearinghouse also were created.

The results?

> *It has been very hard for us to evaluate whether our methods have been successful or not. . . . But I can tell you that in one year we have tripled the number of students who have signed up to join the Peace Corps. . . . In one year we also have quadrupled the number of students who have signed up to go into public-school teaching programs. We look at these as examples of success* (Newman et al. 1985, pp. 11-12).

Law schools, such as Tulane, which require some sort of social service by students, may have reason to do so. According to a report in the *National Law Journal*, in the last five years just 2 per cent of the nation's top law school graduates went directly into public interest positions where they would serve poor and underrepresented people (Mangan 1989a, p. A27).

Furthermore, the lack of law students entering the public service sector appears related more to the effects of the law school experience than students' initial plans when enrolling. At Harvard University, when law students matriculate 35 to 40 percent say they plan a public service career. In reality, at most 4 percent enter either public-interest or government service work directly after graduation (Mangan 1989b, p. A28).

Law school efforts in public service experience
To make public service positions available to interested law students, a number of law schools and the National Association for Public Interest Law (NAPIL) are working to provide financial support. Some law schools are adjusting the payment schedule of graduates who borrowed to attend their schools but now seek to enter public-service jobs.

NAPIL is securing financial support from lawyers, law firms, and law schools to create a fund from which the 40 member institutions can draw to provide service opportunities for students. The fund is used to help students who need a paying summer job to pay for law school and who otherwise could not afford to take public-sector positions.

Such programs have proved highly successful. Sponsoring institutions report that student demand exceeds the available resources to provide the opportunities to serve (Mangan 1989b, p. A28).

The University of California at Berkeley has instituted a loan forgiveness plan. For a small number of graduates who enter community service or take public service jobs, loans from $500 to $2,000 may be canceled. The program is initially planned to operate for two years.

Service in the health field. The health and psychology fields lend themselves to volunteer programming. At the University of Alabama a program has been in existence for 18 years which augments traditional abnormal psychology work with volunteering.

In an Alabama program, students are required to work for 25 hours in a hospital or similar setting. Those who are unable to fulfill this condition do an alternate project such as writing a term paper. Students are assigned to a specific facility where the staff takes full responsibility for what the student does during the period of volunteer work.

. . . just two percent of the nation's top law school graduates went directly into public interest positions where they would serve poor and underrepresented people.

Integration of lectures and readings with volunteer expe-
riences is accomplished by a continued discussion of stu-
dents' reactions to their work during class time (Scogin and
Rickard 1987, pp. 95-96).

While the overall evaluation of the program by students
and staff is positive, "there are several potentially negative
aspects to the volunteer experience for both students and
instructors":

1. First, some students cannot or will not become involved.
2. On occasion a student has experienced psychological conflict when being placed in contact with disturbed adults
   or children.
3. There is a question of liability. This should be explored
   before any program is initiated (Scogin and Rickard 1987,
   p. 96-97).

While students reported "a very positive overall reaction
to the volunteer experience. . . . A somewhat less positive
impact on academic knowledge and motivation was reported"
(Scogin and Rickard 1987, pp. 96-97)

Staff in the psychology department at the University of West
Florida learned from students that they wanted an opportunity
to apply what they were learning. A program was developed
in which students could earn academic credit while volunteering to serve in community agencies and schools. Granting
credit for participation was

based on the research that students are more willing to par-
ticipate in volunteer efforts for academic credits than for
the love of science or even for money (Redfering and Biasco
1982, p. 121).

The program coordinator monitors volunteers' efforts in
the field through student weekly reports which are signed
by the agency supervisor or coordinator. The volunteers also
meet periodically and interact with the course coordinator
about their field experiences. Students are graded "pass" or
"fail" with the credit and notation appearing on the transcript
that the student participated in a practical experience (Redfering and Biasco 1982).

Additional service programs. Colleges in Texas support the Volunteers in Public Schools Program. College students receive credit for working as tutors in the public schools. For education majors this is a valuable hands-on experience; for public school students it provides additional instruction not previously available (Ray 1982, p. 11).

At Norwich University in Northfield, Vt., a two-year program was created for juniors and seniors who wish to serve in the Peace Corps as an alternative to serving in the military. The training includes course work in foreign languages, politics, and the economics of developing countries. Completion of the course does not obligate the student to join the Peace Corps; but those who do join and have loans from Norwich can receive forgiveness for up to $5,000 of their debts.

A growing number of colleges and universities, including Vanderbilt University, Georgetown University, and the College of Wooster have developed volunteer programs as alternatives to the traditional Florida spring break. Students have caught on to the idea, and large numbers are signing up to serve people in need. In some cases students must pay to volunteer, travel to a distant location, pay rent, and purchase meals while working eight to twelve hours a day helping others (Collison 1989b, pp. A33–34).

Collaborative Efforts

Another means of providing volunteer service opportunities for youths comes about through partnership efforts. This occurs when colleges and universities collaborate in various ways with government, business, industry, human service agencies, and other educational institutions (Goodlad 1984, p. 347.)

The Fund for the Improvement of Postsecondary Education (FIPSE) has encouraged community organizations and colleges and universities to create partnerships. FIPSE has provided financial support for several projects aimed at career and educational growth. A sampling of FIPSE projects follows.

- The Red Cross and the Educational Testing Service created a training program. A number of colleges and universities awarded credit to individuals who completed it.
- The National Council of Negro Women, Inc. (NCNW) and Pace University created a program to help black women move from clerical jobs into management, sales, and

administrative positions. Pace provided instructional services while eight major companies conducted task analyses and determined the skills needed for various positions.

- The Lutheran Social Mission Society worked with the Community College of Philadelphia to develop a program for disadvantaged women to go to college.
- In East and West Coast cities nonprofit groups serving blacks, Hispanics, and other minorities worked with area colleges and universities to provide precollege access and preparation programs.
- The National Congress of Neighborhood Women worked to create community-based postsecondary degree programs for females involved in voluntary activities (Stoel 1982, pp. 49–52).

Community organizations

Other partnerships with higher education include those created by Community Based Organizations (CBOs) to educate citizen-members. One such partnership was formed with Beacon College in Norton, Mass. The program's goals are to assist students to acquire a liberal arts education, to increase self-direction, to develop a greater sense of social responsibility, and to think more critically.

Beacon offers majors in community organizing, organizational management, community action, and economic development to accomplish its goals (Rosenman 1982, pp. 74–76).

Brooklyn College, LaGuardia Community College, and Empire State College all worked with the Neighborhood Women in New York City. Both traditional and nontraditional educational programming were provided to low-income individuals. The goals of the programs were to meet the needs identified through the CBOs.

Another program in New York City was created to provide precollegiate educational experiences and opportunities for minority youths. The program used a competency-based approach to assist them in earning a four-year degree and teacher certification.

Other CBO-higher education collaborations were formed in New York City, Birmingham, and Baltimore. They were part of the Clearinghouse of Community Based Free-Standing Educational Institutions which was created by the Association for Community Based Education (Rosenman 1982, pp. 76–79).

Financial Support for Service Programs

Educators and others are concerned that higher education is failing to teach about philanthropy and volunteerism, thus preserving the heritage of this nation. To encourage colleges and universities to focus again on the instruction of civic mindedness and participation, funding is being provided to create model programs. Examples include:

- In 1986 and 1987 the Association of American Colleges gave a total of $150,000 to 16 colleges and universities to develop courses to teach students about philanthropy and its role in shaping American society.

The courses were meant to prepare students for public service and civic responsibility. The grants are part of the association's promotion of the Program on Studying Philanthropy. Several foundations underwrite the program, which operates through the Association of American Colleges (Layton 1987).

- The W. W. Kellogg Foundation gave Albion College a grant of $470,000 to create a model project in volunteering and community action.

- The Ford Foundation gave the Educational Commission of the States $112,000 to support service-work done by college students. It also gave $60,000 to Berea College to study colleges which require students to complete community service before graduation; and it gave the Campus Outreach Opportunity League $25,000 to expand opportunities for students to do community service while in college (*Chronicle of Higher Education* 1987, p. A34).

- The Educational Commission of the States provided funding to both the Campus Outreach Opportunity League (COOL) and the Campus Compact.

These two organizations are actually national networks of colleges and universities working together to increase the voluntary activities of students. Both can provide a variety of services and assistance to institutions of higher education for creating on-campus programming to involve students in civic service.

Campus Outreach Opportunity League

The Campus Outreach Opportunity League (COOL) is a student-organized program working to involve students in community volunteer projects. Its founder, Wayne Meisel, created COOL in 1984, while still a student, by walking 1,500 miles over a nine-month period and stopping at 65 East Coast colleges and universities. Along the way he enlisted students to join a support network of community service volunteer activities.

From that beginning, COOL has grown prodigiously. In 1988 it offered advice on community service to students and staff at more than 450 colleges and universities across the nation. The league was funded initially by a grant from the Hazen Foundation. Since then, COOL has received 10 additional grants as well as assistance and support from its members (Theus 1988, pp. 30, 33).

COOL is, in many ways, the idea of one person; that individual's vision continues to set the tone for the organization. His goal was to go from having 450 campuses to having 1,750 involved with COOL. If his goal is achieved, he will have initiated the equivalent of a billion dollar a year industry, but one that provides civic service.

According to Meisel,

We are developing and fostering a notion of civic partic-
ipation and involvement for the future, a kind of involve-
ment a democratic society like ours is dependent upon
(Theus 1988, p. 33).

The techniques COOL applies to gain support involve staff members as both recruiters and consultants.

They articulate a vision to the converted and proselytize
their students to join the cause of citizen service. Their lit-
erature smacks of Thomas Shepard's Puritanism of righ-
teousness through good works (Theus 1988, p. 33).

The positive tone of the literature published by COOL presents a picture of youth making a difference in communities throughout the nation. Meisel's goal is to link student self-interest to the interests of the needy. "Self-interest, readily understood, is a win-win deal. . . . This whole movement is about complementary needs" (Theus 1988, p. 33).

How COOL recruits students

While the Campus Opportunity Outreach League is idealistic, it is doing things to increase student participation in volunteer activities. For example: Students regularly send the organization information about programs at their respective colleges; they create joint service programs with high schools; and they organize meetings to share information and experiences.

The importance of COOL and similar organizations is the fact that they have students motivating other students. Without students desiring to participate in volunteer activities, "campus administrative structures to support volunteer activity will be of little use" (Theus 1988, pp. 33–36).

Activities. COOL has sponsored a number of activities including a Homeless Teach-in, Literacy Action, and Hunger Clean-Up programs. The hunger program, held in 1987,

> *involved 4,000 students from 116 campuses who completed hundreds of work projects and raised $55,000 in one day for local hunger and homelessness organizations* (Theus 1988, p. 36).

COOL also sponsored the hiring of 40 recent college graduates, or "green deans," to provide leadership in recruiting student volunteers and to direct expanding volunteer service program opportunities at colleges and universities. University administrators praise the green deans for their energy and for making volunteering visible and attractive to more students than if a formalized program did not exist (Collison 1988).

Campus Compact

The Campus Compact—Project for Public and Community Service was founded by Donald Kennedy, president of Stanford University, Rev. Timothy S. Healy, S.J., president of Georgetown University, and Howard R. Swearer, president of Brown University, with the backing of Frank Newman, president of the Education Commission of the States. The educators formed the organization because they believed actions were needed "to stop the denigration of politics, public service, and of those who serve" (Greene 1986, p. 25).

The Campus Compact is a relatively new organization and not fully representative of higher education. It began in 1985 with 12 institutions. By 1990, 225 of almost 3,000 colleges and universities were members. While the organization has made national headlines, that may reflect the membership as well as the growing concern about volunteerism rather than how many students have been involved in Compact projects.

In addition, the high visibility of Compact members such as the Rev. Theodore Hesburgh, president emeritus of the University of Notre Dame, is expected to draw other campus leaders into membership (Collison 1990, p. A35.)

The Campus Compact is a project of the Education Commission of the States. Its plan is to alter the environment at colleges and universities so that volunteerism becomes an integral part of the undergraduate education. Frank Newman, the Commission's president,

> *believes that higher-education institutions have a responsibility for promoting civic-mindedness among their students, and that the apathy of today's generation is in part the fault of educators who have not placed enough emphasis on public-service values* (Greene 1987, pp. 32).

During 1986-87 the Campus Compact assisted colleges and universities in a number of ways including technical help and written materials. It also created the Center for Public Service at Brown University, held regional workshops, and provided expertise to member institutions through on-site visits.

The Compact secured funding from foundations and corporations. It also worked with Senator Pell to develop a voluntary national service bill, and with the State Initiatives Task Force (that works with state legislators) to develop innovative legislative proposals and to foster voluntary activities on college campuses.

In addition, the Compact worked with members of Congress to encourage the creation of a link between public service and financial aid programs. This led to an amendment which increased the federal contribution to the College Work-Study Program when students work in community service programs.

The Compact also secured internships for students to work in the Peace Corps for 10 and 15 weeks, found ways for students to be involved with the Project Literacy U.S. (PLUS), and formed coalitions with other national organizations (Campus Compact 1987; Greene 1987).

The Campus Compact published a report of the activities

of 67-member institutions from information they provided. Seventeen members enroll more than 10,000 students. All the respondents have programs involving students in all types of voluntary activities, both on and off campus.

In addition to opportunities for student involvement, 36 institutions make opportunities available to staff, and 28 do so for faculty. Forty-five of the institutions provide an information clearinghouse of opportunities for public service in both the community and government, and 54 of the colleges and universities provide internships.

Half of the 67 institutions provide work-study and other types of financial assistance for service work; more than half provide job placement services for students seeking public service careers. Fifty-six schools grant academic credit for experiential learning activities with a service orientation. Thirty-four institutions have established centers to encourage public service, and a majority of those have a paid staff (Ventresca et al. 1987, pp. 1–6).

Campus Compact evaluation

For all the efforts, however, participation was not at a desired level. While 70 percent of the colleges and universities responding said they had at least 100 students involved in service activities, only 27 institutions (40 percent) had more than 500 students actively volunteering in 1985-86.

When asked why students did not participate in greater numbers, member institutions listed such reasons as finances, career considerations, lack of academic credit, lack of information, and diminished support of public service (Ventresca et al. 1987, pp. 8–9).

Two years later an article in *The New York Times* indicated that at Yale, 2,200 of 5,100 undergraduates volunteered for community service, while at Harvard the percent who were involved had gone from 33 percent in 1983 to 60 percent (Theus 1988, p. 31).

Finances

The Campus Compact was instrumental in getting the Fund for the Improvement of Postsecondary Education to create a special program, "Innovative Projects for Student Community Service," and to appropriate $1.5 million for community service projects. FIPSE gave some 25 awards of $10,000 to $70,000 for one to two years to colleges and universities as well as to other private and public nonprofit organizations. The funds supported projects that encouraged students to participate in community service activities (Grant Alert 1988, p. 5; and Greene 1987, p. 32.).

Foundations consider the Campus Compact a catalyst. Support includes gifts from the Arco Foundation, which gave $20,000, and the Andrew W. Mellon Foundation, which gave $260,000 (*Chronicle of Higher Education* 1987, p. A26).

State campus compacts

The Campus Compact currently is expanding through the creation of state-wide compacts. The first two State Compacts were in Pennsylvania and Michigan. The third is the California Compact which "will include the chancellors and presidents of University of California and California State University campuses, as well as private and community colleges" (Greene 1988, p. A31).

There are several reasons for creating state-wide compacts including the opportunity to unite to offer more comprehensive programming for involving faculty and students in service activities.

Educator Frank Newman hopes the creation of state Compacts will continue. He is concerned that the group of 140 colleges belonging to the national Campus Compact is reaching a size that does not permit close working relationships. In his view, state-forged compacts have the potential to offer more services and draw more institutions into participation (Greene 1988, pp. A31–A32).

Susan Stroud, director of Campus Compact, is convinced that the college presidents have provided, and will continue to provide, the greatest amount of leadership to create service programming on campuses. They have provided funding, faculty release time, and worked with legislators and others to create an entire new ethic and interest in community service. The work of college presidents, she thinks, far exceeds what any bill passed by Congress could ever achieve because they have stimulated many diverse activities (Stroud 1989, p. 4).

Summary

The Campus Compact is involved in a growing number of projects at colleges and universities, as well as state-wide initiatives. It offers a variety of support services to institutions wishing to create service programs. Both The Campus Compact and the Campus Outreach Opportunity League are meant to involve entire institutions in service activities.

Faculty Participation

Students are finding that volunteering provides an opportunity to do something they can believe in and that their ideas are valued. But faculty do not have the same positive outlook on service programming (Newman et al. 1985).

> The public has been extremely interested in this effort [to institute service programming]. The faculty has been extremely negative. Not all the faculty, of course, but the general reaction has been, 'This isn't any of our business. Students aren't here to get into these frivolous things like learning citizenship and becoming able to function in American society' (Newman et al. 1985, p. 13).

Faculty expect students to learn the subjects they teach in their courses. When questioned about values, according to Newman, faculty say, "None of that ideological indoctrination in my class." People have repeatedly said, "'This isn't a function of higher education'—forgetting that the original function of education in this country was for the development of civic leadership." A major task facing those who believe that volunteer programs should be offered by higher education is "...to convince the faculties of this country that they've got to change their ways on this issue" (Newman et al. 1985, p. 13).

Faculty may have to make changes in how they approach their jobs to become supportive of the concept of students volunteering as part of their education. Learning teamwork and leadership skills are not opportunities provided by most current curricula. Nor do current faculty personnel practices or pedagogical techniques encourage the development of trust, empathy, and cooperation.

Twenty years of research indicates that students are much more interested in status, power, and money and much less concerned with contributing to their communities or helping others.

> It's almost as if students are aping their professors and their institutions by emphasizing competition and individualism over cooperation and teamwork (Astin 1987, p. 18).

Learning teamwork and leadership skills are not opportunities provided by most current curricula.

To alter the current environment of education from one focused on competition to one focused on cooperation will require a number of changes. Faculty and staff need to examine

> *the way we teach our classes, treat our students, and treat our colleagues. And when we have an opportunity to participate in curriculum decisions, long-range planning, and similar kinds of group activities, we can take the initiative to introduce value questions such as 'cooperation versus competition' into the deliberations* (Astin 1987, pp. 18–19).

Faculty participation, administrative support, and the creation of courses and programs to increase civic participation can be a positive step in preserving this nation's heritage. Once in place, however, how can it be determined if such coursework, programming, and service activities alter the characteristics of contemporary youth? Will their attitudes, values, and abilities be changed? And if so, how will those changes be measured?

Evaluating the Effects of Civic Participation

Learning seems to move from the concrete to the abstract. The unquestioning trust of youth vanishes over time, giving way to a more critical analysis of systems, events, and people. This change requires more than individual maturation; it requires various influences to help mold students' knowledge and opinions. Influences include parents, peers, schools, and the media. Each plays a role in the formulation of youths' feelings and knowledge about society.

Part of the process is seeking the attitudes of people known for political information. Relying on the media is part of this growth process. But decisions regarding citizenship require more (Zevin 1983, pp. 120–23).

At the heart of the matter is how a person views citizenship and the political process. Can a person conceptualize, make decisions, and focus on abstract topics? Or does a person make snap judgments based on personal feelings and incomplete knowledge? Actions reflect the individual's cognitive development.

What studies tell us

The results of one study found that college students who are more tolerant have a more abstract and broader view of citizenship, acknowledge majority rule and minority rights for specific groups, support political conflicts as legitimate, see citizenship defined in an active sense, and believe they need to actively participate in society. The less tolerant the students are, the more passive they conceive the role of a citizen to be.

> *If, as a cognitive developmental theoretical perspective implies, the capacity for conflict tolerance is limited by the level of cognitive moral development attained by the individual, then it is crucial for the development of citizen competence for educators to facilitate this intellectual growth* (Eyler 1980, p. 23).

Educational outcomes

The kind of educational outcomes people look for from a college education can be many, depending on who the person is and what the person seeks. These outcomes include: employment, professional productivity, personal happiness, increased knowledge, greater skills, and the ability to make decisions.

In the personal development of an individual what counts is the capacity for moral judgment and logical thought. In the maturation process, youth may reject their elders' values, but often have no others to put in their place because they have not yet developed them.

Volunteer activities offer the opportunity for the development of values and decision-making skills because participation requires the individual to take actions which cause cognitive development in these two areas. As volunteers, students assume responsibility for others as well as for themselves. They must make decisions, act on those decisions, and live with the results (Graham 1973, pp. 186–88).

Accepting the responsibility to foster the development of logical thinking and moral judgment means two things for higher education.

- First, methods to teach these must be created.
- Second, methods to determine whether there is growth in these two areas must be applied.

The first can be accomplished by changing curricula and by getting students to participate in volunteer activities. The latter is not as easily done, for several reasons.

1. In order to determine whether students gain from experiences, the demands and expectations of the voluntary activities must match the skills, interests, and abilities of the student volunteers. For logic and value development, success may be best achieved if students are challenged at a level, or stage, above their current development.
2. This requires that students have the opportunity to be taught, to become co-participants, and ultimately to be co-leaders. The development of one's ego, aesthetic judgment, expression, and leadership abilities all go into the growth of one's skills in logical thinking and moral decision making. No development will take place when students are put in positions where the challenges do not require growth, the exertion of ability, or thought.
3. An evaluation of the students' abilities must be done to determine if students have any gains from specific educational experiences. The development of students' logical thought and judgment skills can be measured using evaluative tools applied as pre- and post-experience measurement devices (Graham 1973, pp. 188–92).

Measurement techniques

Measuring the outcomes of experiential or service learning with a strong component of social participation must include more than pencil and paper methods of evaluation, especially if measurement is to determine partially political content outcomes. Multiple measurement methods should be used to assess each outcome due to little previous research on which to build an evaluation program.

It is advantageous to use standardized, reliable, and valid instruments to test for results to compare those results to ones from other programs. In testing the effects of experiential programs, a variety of instruments and other methods of gathering information can be used including validated instruments, observation, and self-kept logs. Follow-up studies can be conducted to learn if the changes were temporary or carried over for a length of time (Hedin and Conrad 1980, pp. 10–11).

Evaluation may be viewed by some as a final step in altering the curriculum and instituting experiential programs meant to involve students in volunteering. Those proposing the legislation of a national service program are coming to their conclusions by evaluating contemporary youth and U.S. social problems. The question is, will higher education take action to change curricula and institute service programming without waiting for the evaluation to be completed?

CONCLUSIONS AND RECOMMENDATIONS

Higher education is acting to alter curricula and institute a variety of programs to provide students the opportunity to become involved in the civic arena. National organizations are in place to aid the effort, and financial support is available. Nonetheless, those in support of student volunteer programs criticize the actions as inadequate.

Problems that Need Solving

Even if higher education institutes new programs and expands existing ones on the local and state level, it may be that the move to create a formal national service program has too much impetus and support to be turned back. Support for federally legislated national service seems to be growing each year; even the President of the United States has a proposal to create a volunteer program. At the same time, several questions remain.

1. If President Bush implements his proposed national service program, how will it be funded? How will any effort to create a national service program be funded at a time when the national debt is so great?

Some experts feel that taxes will have to be increased unless Congress cuts a variety of expenditures from the national budget. Neither appears likely; and even if taxes are raised, it is questionable if enough money will be taken from existing budget items to fund a national service program of any significant size.

2. Even if funding is available to create a national service program, would all youth be required to serve? Or would participation be by choice?

Programs operating out of conscription raise several concerns.

Risks of misassignment, poor supervision, poor performance, costs of administration, and (in compulsory plans) costs of enforcement also need to be considered (Theus 1988, p. 37).

Those risks also apply to programs run at the local or institutional level, but it is possible that greater control can be exercised over a program which is institutionally based compared to one that is national in scope.

In examining what and who would be served in a mandatory system, the costs in dollars, morale, performance, motivation, and loss of personal liberty may outweigh the social benefits national service offers (Theus 1988, p. 37).

Students serving because they "have" to may provide inadequate services, create problems for those they serve as well as themselves, and undermine the program. On the other hand, a voluntary program which offers incentives could mean that "only groups interested in the incentives would apply, potentially deepening economic and social divisions in society" (Theus 1988, p. 37).

This could be true especially if the benefits were vouchers to attend college. "Educational loans currently serve several million students, as compared to the DLC [Democratic Leadership Council] service corps target of 700,000" (Theus 1988, p. 38). And yet the Democrats' proposal includes doing away with grants and loans for anyone who does not serve.

3. Finally, there is the definition of volunteerism followed in this monograph which depends on students freely choosing volunteer service. How will the definition apply to those who serve in a program which requires participation?

If someone is required to volunteer, the idea behind volunteer service is taken away. That is, one volunteers by choosing to do so, not because it is required. The programs at most colleges and universities are elective. The number of institutions of higher education which require a period of service for graduation are very small (Theus 1988).

As many educators and students have said, today's youth are not as selfish as they are perceived; they just need the opportunity to volunteer.

Proposals for Higher Education

- Colleges and universities need to conduct a thorough evaluation of their graduation requirements. This should include their guidelines for graduation as well as the recommendations of reports made about the conditions of higher education in America.

- Higher education institutions then should change their graduation requirements to include: courses to expose students to the traditions of the liberal arts; courses that will lead students to think, react, and make decisions; experiential learning opportunities to expose them to all aspects of society through participation.

By initiating such requirements for graduation, higher education will take great strides to bring civic consciousness back to youth.

- Colleges and universities need to work together to create national service opportunities for their students.

Programs could be centered on individual campuses, involve a group of colleges, or be regional, even national, in scope. In all programming, a wide variety of service opportunities should be made available. But simply making them available is not enough.

- Service placements must match the skills and interest of both the students and the requirements of the positions.

The institution has a responsibility to provide full placement services. This requires job analysis, student skill analysis, and a close working relationship with agencies and their personnel. Placement must be followed by monitoring the performance of students while they carry out their duties, and it must end with an evaluation and summary report made available to the students.

The total process should be a positive educational experience. To accomplish these goals, a course or other opportunity for feedback and discussion while the students are serving also should be provided.

- Students also must be given the opportunity to learn about the nonprofit sector.

Courses and research should be done to expand information about the independent sector and support for its activities. Students need to learn about the history of this nation's citizens volunteering for the well-being of others. Students need to be exposed to philanthropy, understand what being altruistic means, and learn that being a donor of both money and time for the welfare of those in need is expected, worthwhile, and pays rewards.

- Service programming requires funding, and it is to the benefit of colleges and universities to seek foundation, individual, and government support to create voluntary programs, introduce new courses, and restructure the curriculum.

- Restructuring and the creation of new programs also means that faculty and staff need to become involved as participatory citizens.

Faculty set examples, as do administrators. College and university leaders need to recognize and encourage the involvement of all members of their communities in civic activities, research of the independent sector, and in providing leadership to students.

Summary

What will it take to attain the goal of imbuing youth with an understanding of civic responsibility? It requires that each person join forces with others, and that each organization become a part of many who desire to see youth become involved at the civic level. It also requires higher education to take the lead in organizing and providing opportunities for college students to participate in service programs.

REFERENCES

The Educational Resources Information Center (ERIC) Clearinghouse on Higher Education abstracts and indexes the current literature on higher education for inclusion in ERIC's data base and announcement in ERIC's monthly bibliographic journal, *Resources in Education* (RIE). Most of these publications are available through the ERIC Document Reproduction Service (EDRS). For publications cited in this bibliography that are available from EDRS, ordering number and price code are included. Readers who wish to order a publication should write to the ERIC Document Reproduction Service, 7420 Fullerton Rd., Suite 110, Springfield, VA 22153-2852. (Phone orders with VISA or MasterCard are taken at 800-443-ERIC or 703-440-1400.) When ordering, please specify the document (ED) number. Documents are available as noted in microfiche (MF) and paper copy (PC). If you have the price code ready when you call EDRS, an exact price can be quoted. The last page of the latest issue of *Resources in Education* also has the current cost, listed by code.

Astin, Alexander. September/October 1987. "Competition or Cooperation? Teaching Teamwork as a Basic Skill." *Change* 19: 12–19.

Astin, Alexander; Green, Kenneth C.; and Korn, William S. 1987. *The American Freshman: Twenty Year Trends.* Los Angeles: University of California.

Balderston, Frederick E. 1978. *Managing Today's University.* San Francisco: Jossey-Bass.

Bernstein, Alison. September/October 1985. "Goodbye Mr. Chips?" *Change.* 17: 6–7.

Blumenstyk, Goldie. 22 March 1989. "State Leaders Are Wary of Federal Efforts to Line Student Aid to Volunteer Service." *Chronicle of Higher Education.* 35: A1, A20.

Bok, Derek. "Prepared Statement of Derek Bok, President, Harvard University." In *Reauthorization of Title I of the Domestic Volunteer Service Act of 1973.* Hearing for House Committee on Education and Labor, Subcommittee on Select Education. 99th Congress. Feb. 26, 1986. 33–36. ED 273 807 104 pp. MF–01; PC–05.

Bowen, Howard R., and Schuster, Jack H. 1986. *American Professors: A National Source Imperiled.* New York: Oxford University Press.

Boyer, Ernest L. 1986. *College: The Undergraduate Experience in America.* Princeton, N.J.: The Carnegie Foundation for the Advancement of Teaching.

Boyer, Ernest L. and Hechinger, Fred M. 1981. *Higher Learning in the Nation's Service.* Washington, D.C.: Carnegie Foundation for the Advancement of Teaching. ED 212 206. 75 pp. MF–01; PC not available EDRS.

Campus Compact. 1987. *Summary of Campus Compact's Activities in '86-'87 to Increase College Student Involvement in Public and Community Service.* Providence, R.I.: Brown University. Campus Compact: The Project for Public and Community Service. A Project of the Education Commission of the States.

Carnegie Foundation for the Advancement of Teaching. September/ October 1985. "Change Trendlines. The Faculty: Deeply Troubled." *Change.* 17: 31–35.

Chalmers, David. September 1984. "Committed, Proud, and Distrustful: The Mississippi Freedom Volunteers 20 Years Later." *USA Today* 113: 36–39.

Chronicle of Higher Education. 12 August 1987. "'Literacy Corps' to Train Students to Teach." 33: A2.

———. 9 September 1987. "Private Gifts and Grants to Higher Education." 34: A30.

———. 16 September 1987. "Norwich Offers Students Training for Peace Corps." 34: A2.

———. 14 October 1987. "Private Grants and Gifts to Higher Education." 34: A34.

———. 25 November 1987. "Private Grants and Gifts to Higher Education." 34: A26.

———. 17 February 1988. "Berkeley to Forgive Loans for Community Service." 34: A2.

Coalition for National Service. 1988. *National Service: An Action Agenda for the 1990s.* Washington, D.C.: National Service Secretariat.

Collison, Michelle. 30 November 1988. "Colleges Hire Young Graduates, Dubbed 'Green Deans,' to Help Run Their Student- Volunteer Programs." *Chronicle of Higher Education.* 35: A33, A36.

———. 22 March 1989a. "Students at Conference Question Proposal to Link Aid and Service." *Chronicle of Higher Education.* 34: A32–34.

———. 22 March 1989b. "For Some Students Spring Break Offers Chance to Aid the Needy." *Chronicle of Higher Education.* 35: A33–34.

———. 24 January 1990. "A New Face is Seen for Activism in 1990s: 'Pragmatic Idealism.'" *Chronicle of Higher Education.* 36: A31, A35.

Commission on Private Philanthropy and Public Needs. 1975. "The Third Sector." In *Giving in America: Toward a Stronger Voluntary Sector.* 31–52. Washington, D.C.: Commission on Private Philanthropy and Public Needs.

Committee for the Study of National Service. January 1979. *Youth and the Needs of the Nation.* Washington, D.C.: Potomac Institute.

Crosson, Patricia H. 1983. *Public Service in Higher Education: Practices and Priorities.* ASHE-ERIC Higher Education Report No. 7. Washington, D.C.: Association for the Study of Higher Education. ED 239 569. 140 pp. MF–01; PC–06.

Danzig, Richard, and Szanton, Peter. 1986. *National Service: What Would It Mean?* Lexington, Mass.: Lexington Books of D. C. Heath and Company.

DeLoughry, Thomas J. 2 August 1989. "Washington Update." *Chronicle of Higher Education.* 35: A16.

DeLoughry, Thomas J., and Myers, Christopher. 28 June 1989. "Bush Proposes $25 Million to Coordinate Community-Service Efforts." *Chronicle of Higher Education.* 35: A14, A19.

Dodge, Susan. 24 January 1990. "More Freshmen Willing to Work for Social Change and Environmental Issues, New Survey Finds." *Chronicle of Higher Education.* 36: A31–34.

Dolan, Timothy. 1986. "National Service as a Non-School Alternative to Education at the Secondary-Postsecondary Interface." Paper presented at the Western Region Conference of the Comparative and International Education Society, December, Manoa, Hawaii. ED 277 142. 25 pp. MF–01; PC–01.

Eberly, Donald J. January 1984. "National Service: An Issue For the Eighties." *NASSP Bulletin* 68: 44–51.

———. May 1985. "Youth Service Initiatives: A Promise for the Future." *NASSP Bulletin* 69: 82–88.

Eberly, Donald J., and Sherraden, Michael, W. 1982a. "National Service Precedents in the United States." In *National Service: Social, Economic, and Military Impacts,* edited by Michael W. Sherraden and Donald J. Eberly. Pergamon Policy Studies. New York: Pergamon Press.

———. 1982b. "Alternative Models of National Service." In *National Service: Social, Economic, and Military Impacts,* edited by Michael W. Sherraden and Donald J. Eberly. Pergamon Policy Studies. New York: Pergamon Press.

———. 1982c. "National Service at Launch Point." In *National Service: Social, Economic, and Military Impacts,* edited by Michael W. Sherraden and Donald J. Eberly. Pergamon Policy Studies. New York: Pergamon Press.

Eisenberg, Pablo. 1977. "The Voluntary Sector: Problems and Changes." In *Research Papers,* 2(1). Commission on Private Philanthropy and Public Needs. Washington, D.C.: Department of the Treasury.

Evangelauf, Jean. 7 January 1987a. "Students' Borrowing Quintuples in Decade, Raising the Specter of a 'Debtor Generation'" *Chronicle of Higher Education* 33: 1, 18–25.

———. 2 December 1987b. "Student Financial Aid Reaches $20.5-Billion, but Fails to Keep Pace with Rising College Costs, Study Finds." *Chronicle of Higher Education* 34: A33, A36.

Eyler, Janet. Summer 1980. "Citizenship Education for Conflict: An Empirical Assessment of the Relationship between Principled Thinking and Tolerance for Conflict and Diversity." *Theory and Research in Social Education* 8: 11–26.

Fitch, R. Thomas. 1987. "Characteristics and Motivations of College Students Volunteering for Community Service." *Journal of College Student Personnel.* 28: 424–431.

Floro, George K. Fall 1985. "A Voluntary Sector for Philanthropy and Volunteerism." *Wisconsin Sociologist* 22: 161–72.

Ford, William D. 15 March 1989. "Bill in Congress on Public Service for Young People Shows Confusion About Student Aid and Patriotism." *Chronicle of Higher Education.* 35: A40.

Futter, Ellen V. Spring 1986. "Toward a More Informed Electorate." *Kettering Review* 46–52.

Gardner, John W. 1983. "The Independent Sector." In *America's Voluntary Spirit: A Book of Readings*, edited by Brian O'Connell. New York: The Foundation Center.

Giroux, Henry A. Spring 1987. "Citizenship, Public Philosophy, and the Struggle for Democracy." *Educational Theory* 37: 103–120.

Goodlad, John I. 1984. *A Place Called School: Prospects for the Future.* New York: McGraw-Hill.

Graham, Richard A. 1973. "Voluntary Action and Experiential Education." *Journal of Voluntary Action Research* 2: 186–193.

Grant Alert. October 1988. *The Campus Compact Newsletter.*

Green, Kenneth C., and Astin, Alexander W. Winter 1985. "The Mood on Campus: More Conservative or Just More Materialistic?" *Educational Record* 66: 45–48.

Greene, Elizabeth. 22 January 1986. "University Presidents Urged to Boost the Quality of Student Volunteerism as Well as the Amount." *Chronicle of Higher Education* 31: 25.

———. 21 January 1987. "'Campus Compact' Project Stresses Public Service Commitment by Students." *Chronicle of Higher Education* 33: 1, 32.

———. 7 December 1988. "Organization to Promote Public Service by Students Formed by California Higher-Education Leaders." *Chronicle of Higher Education.* 35: A31–32.

Greenberg, Elinor M. December 1982. "Reaching Out and Looking Up: A New Model for Partnerships." In *New Partnerships: Higher Education and the Nonprofit Sector*, edited by Elinor M. Greenberg. New Directions for Experiential Learning No. 18. San Francisco: Jossey-Bass.

Griffith, Pat. 1 February 1989. "Congress gets 2nd Youth Service Bill. *The Blade* 4.

Guardo, Carol, J. April 1982. "Student Generations and Value Change." *Personnel and Guidance Journal* 60: 500–03, 35–39.

Hartle, Terry W., and Taylor, John. August/September 1985. "What's Big on Campus?" *Public Opinion* 8: 49–53.

Hedin, Diane. 1982. "The Views of Adolescents and Young Adults on Civic Obligations and National Service." In *National Service: Social, Economic, and Military Impacts,* edited by Michael W. Sherraden and Donald J. Eberly. Pergamon Policy Studies. New York: Pergamon Press.

Hedin, Diane, and Conrad, Dan. 1980. "Study Proves Hypotheses—and More." *Synergist* 9: 8–14.

Hepburn, Mary A. November/December 1985. "What Is Our Youth Thinking? Social-Political Attitudes of the 1980s." *Social Education* 49: 671–77.

Hirschorn, Michael, W. 20 January 1988. "Freshman Interest in Business Careers Hits New Level, and Money Remains a Top Priority, Study Finds." *Chronicle of Higher Education* 34: A31, A34–37.

Hodgkinson, Virginia A., and Weitzman, Murray S. 1988. *Giving and Volunteering in The United States: Findings form A National Survey.* Washington, D.C.: Independent Sector.

Hogan, Harry J. 1981. "Philosophic Issues in Volunteerism." *Journal of Voluntary Action Research* 10: 90–10

Ivory, Shanda Thomas. 14 August 1989. "Interview." *Higher Education & National Affairs.* 38: 6.

Karl, Barry D. 1983. "Corporate Philanthropy: Historical Background." In *Corporate Philanthropy.* Washington, D.C.: Council on Foundations.

Kennedy, Donald. 1986. "'Can We Help?' Public Service and the Young." Paper presented at the annual meeting of the American Association for Higher Education, March, Washington, D.C. ED 270 001. 10pp. MF–01; PC–01.

Kramer, Martin A., and Van Dusen, William D. May/June 1986. "Living On Credit." *Change.* 18: 10–19.

Kuntz, Phil. 25 March 1989. "Nunn-McCurdy Plan Ignites National Service Debate." *Congressional Quarterly.* 645–48.

Landrum, Roger. January 1979. "Service to Society: The Missing Dimension for American Youth." *Youth and the Needs of the Nation.* Report of the Committee for the Study of National Service. Washington, D.C.: The Potomac Institute.

Layton, Daphne. N. 28, October 1987. "AAC Awards $105,000 More for Courses on Philanthropy." *News.* Washington, D.C.: Association of American Colleges.

Levine, Arthur. 1980. *When Dreams and Heroes Died: A Portrait of Today's College Student.* San Francisco: Jossey-Bass.

————. April 1986. "Hearts and Minds: The Freshman Challenge." *Bulletin* 38: 3–6.

MacArthur, Robert S. Fall 1985. "The Stranger Without and the Stranger Within . . . Transplanting the Liberal Heart." *Journal of Experiential Education* 8: 6–12.

Mangan, Katherine S. 1 February 1989a. "Law Schools Expect a Record Number of Applicants, But Interest in Public Service Jobs May be Waning." *Chronicle of Higher Education.* 25: A27–28.

————. 1 February 1989b. "Some Programs Make Low-Paying Legal Jobs Attractive." *Chronicle of Higher Education.* 35: A28.

Mayville, William V. 1980. "Changing Perspectives on the Urban College and University." AAHE-ERIC Higher Education Research Currents. Washington, D.C.: ERIC Clearing House on Higher Education. ED 185 890. 5 pp. MF–01; PC–01.

McCartan, Annie-Marie. September/October 1988. "Students Who Work: Are They Paying Too High A Price?" *Change.* 20: 11–20.

McMillen, Liz. 21 October 1987. "Colleges Urged to Instill 'Charitable Impulse' in Students, Inspire Them to Reorient Public Policy as Well as Donate Their Time and Money." *Chronicle of Higher Education* 34: A33–A34.

———. 26 October 1988. "Top Executives Found Pessimistic on Future of Corporate Giving." *Chronicle of Higher Education.* 35: A37–38.

Moskos, Charles C. 1988. *A Call To Civic Service: National Service for Country and Community.* New York: Free Press.

Myers, Christopher. 19 April 1989. "Student Leaders on National Service." *Chronicle of Higher Education.* 35: A22.

National Commission on the Role and Future of State Colleges and Universities. 1986. *To Secure The Blessings of Liberty.* Washington, D.C.: American Association of State Colleges and Universities.

National Service Secretariat. April 1987. "Bumpers, Pell, McCurdy, Panetta, Torricelli, and Udall Introduce National Service Legislation." *National Service Newsletter* 50: 1, 4.

———. March 1988. "Support For National Service Reaches Record High of 83%." *National Service Newsletter.* 52: 2.

———. October 1988. "Youth Service Corps Bill Advances: Sen. Nunn Promotes Citizens Corps." *National Service Newsletter.* 53: 2.

———. March 1989. "Bumpers, Dodd, Kennedy, Kennelly, McCain, McCurdy, Mikulski, Mitchell, Morella, Nunn, Panetta, Pell, Sikorski, Udall Propose Varied Forms of National Youth Service." *National Service Newsletter.* 54: 1–2.

———. March 1990. "Senate Passes $125 Million National Service Bill." *National Service Newsletter.* 56: 1–3.

Neiman, Judith. May 1988. "State Initiatives. Youth Service: The Big Picture." *Campus Compact Newsletter.* 2: 3.

Newman, Frank. 1985. *Higher Education and the American Resurgence.* Princeton, N.J.: Carnegie Foundation for the Advancement of Teaching. ED 265 759. 282 pp. MF–01; PC not available EDRS.

———. July/August 1987. "Students In Public Service: Honoring Those Who Care." *Change* 19: 19–27.

———. September/October 1989. "National Policies to Encourage Service: Where Do We Stand?" *Change.* 21: 9–17.

Newman, Frank; Milton, Catherine; and Stroud, Susan. June 1985. "Community Service and Higher Education: Obligations and Opportunities." *Bulletin* 37: 9–13.

Newsletter of the American Council on Education. 13 February 1989a. "Volunteer Service Bills Introduced." *Higher Education & National Affairs.* 38: 1, 4.

———. 13 March 1989b. "Whalen to Testify on National Service." *Higher Education & National Affairs.* 38: 1–2.

———. 14 August 1989c. "Service Measure Gains in Senate." *Higher*

Education & National Affairs. 38: 1–2.

O'Connell, Brian. 1982. "The Independent Sector: Uniquely American" In *New Partnerships: Higher Education and the Nonprofit Sector*, edited by Elinor M. Greenberg. New Directions for Experiential Learning No. 18. San Francisco: Jossey-Bass.

"Opinion Roundup." February/March 1982. *Public Opinion* 5: 21–31.

Pifer, Alan. 1984. *Philanthropy in an Age of Transition.* New York: Foundation Center.

———. Winter 1987. "Philanthropy, Voluntarism, and Changing Times." *Daedalus* 118: 119–132.

Ramsay, William R. 1982. "The Impact of National Service on Education." In National Service. Social, Economic and Military Impacts, edited by Michael W. Sherraden and Donald J. Eberly, (pp. 135-149). Pergamon Policy Studies. New York: Pergamon Press.

Ray, Garrett W. 1982. "Meeting Volunteers on their own Ground" In *New Partnerships: Higher Education and the Nonprofit Sector*, edited by Elinor M. Greenberg. New Directions for Experiential Learning No. 18. San Francisco: Jossey-Bass.

Redfering, David L., and Biasco, Frank. Summer 1982. "Volunteering For College Credit." *College Student Journal* 121–123.

Reichlin, Seth. 1982. "Volunteering and Adult Education: A Historical View." In *New Partnerships: Higher Education and the Nonprofit Sector*, edited by Elinor M. Greenberg. New Directions for Experiential Learning No. 18. San Francisco: Jossey-Bass.

Riesman, David. 1976. "Some Questions about Discontinuities in American Society." In *The Uses of Controversy in Sociology*, edited by Lewis A. Coser and Otto N. Larsen. New York: Free Press.

Robb, Governor Charles. June 1985. "Community Service and Higher Education: A National Agenda." *Bulletin* 37: 3–5, 7–8.

Rosenman, Mark. December 1982. "Colleges and Social Change: Partnerships with Community-Based Organizations." In *New Partnerships: Higher Education and the Nonprofit Sector*, edited by Elinor M. Greenberg. New Directions for Experiential Learning No. 18. San Francisco: Jossey-Bass.

Rudolph, Frederick. 1962. *The American College and University: A History.* New York: Alfred A. Knopf.

Rushton, J. Philippe. April 1982. "Altruism and Society: A Social Learning Perspective." *Ethics* 92: 425–46.

Scogin, Forrest, and Rickard, Henry C. 1987. "A Volunteer Program for Abnormal Psychology Students: Eighteen Years and Still Going Strong." *Teaching of Psychology.* 14: 95–97.

Sherraden, Michael W., and Eberly, Donald J. 1982. "Why National Service?" In *National Service. Social, Economic, and Military Impacts*, edited by Michael W. Sherraden and Donald J. Eberly. Pergamon Policy Studies. New York: Pergamon Press.

Slaughter, John B. 16 October 1985. "The Inaugural Address." In *The*

Inauguration Addresses. Toledo, Ohio: University of Toledo.

Special Change Roundtable Interview. September/October 1985. "In Pursuit of Commitment." *Change.* 17: 45–50.

Staff Reporter. 12 November 1986. "Nine Colleges Get Grants to Start Courses Relating to Philanthropy." *Chronicle of Higher Education* 33: 38.

Steckmest, Francis W., with Business Roundtable Resource and Review Committee. 1982. *Corporate Performance: The Key to Public Trust.* New York: McGraw-Hill.

Stoel, Carol F. December 1982. "Improving Postsecondary Education Through the Nonprofit Sector." In *New Partnerships: Higher Education and the Nonprofit Sector,* edited by Elinor M. Greenberg. New Directions for Experiential Learning No. 18. San Francisco: Jossey-Bass.

Stroud, Susan. September/October 1989. "Toward a New Ethic of Service." *Change.* 21: 4.

Swager, Robert G. Spring 1985. "Service-Learning: A Model for Educational Volunteers." *Focus on Learning* 11: 115–19.

Swearer, Howard. June 1985. "Community Service and Higher Education: A National Agenda." *Bulletin* 37: 5–8.

Theus, Kathryn T. September/October 1988. "Campus-Based Community Service: New Populism or 'Smoke and Mirrors'?" *Change.* 20: 26–38.

Thompson, Irene T. Summer 1985. "From Other-Direction to the Me Decade: The Development of Fluid Identities and Personal Role Definitions." *Sociological Inquiry* 55: 274–90.

Torralba, Veronica. April 1988. "At-Risk Youth: Battling the Crisis with a National Mentoring Program." *Campus Compact Newsletter.* 2: 1, 7.

Van Til, Jon. Spring 1985. "Voluntarism." *Social Policy* 15: 28–31.

Ventresca, Marc J.; Waring, Anna L; Halleck, Jeanne W.;;Baker, Saphira M; and Auchard, Melissa. January 1987. *Collegiate Community Service: Status of Public and Community Service at Selected Colleges and Universities.* Providence, R.I.: Brown University.

Voluntarism in America: Promoting Individual and Corporate Responsibility. Hearing before the Subcommittee on Aging, Family and Human Services of the Committee on Labor and Human Resources, U.S. Senate, 97th Congress, 2nd Session (April 22, 1982). Washington, D.C.: Senate Committee on Labor and Human Resources. ED 224 973. 152 pp. MF–01; PC not available EDRS.

Voluntary National Youth Service Act and the Select Commission on National Service Opportunities Act of 1985. Hearing before the Subcommittee on Employment Opportunities of the Committee on Education and Labor, United States House of Representatives, 96th Congress, 1st Session on HR 888 and HR 1326 (Sept. 27, 1985). Washington, D.C.: House Committee on Education and Labor. ED 267 165. 240pp. MF–01; PC–10.

Wagner, Jon. September/October 1987. "Teaching and Research as Student Responsibilities: Integrating Community and Academic Work." *Change* 19: 26–35.

Wilson, Robin. 25 January 1989a. "Lawmakers Expect a Struggle Over Plan That Would Link Federal Student Aid to Community or Military Service." *Chronicle of Higher Education.* 35: A20–A21, A24.

————. 15 February 1989b. "'Indentured Servitude': Many College Officials Oppose Plan that Would Require National Service as a Prerequisite for Federal Student Aid...But Some Student Leaders Approve of the Idea of Public Service." *Chronicle of Higher Education.* 35: A19, A24.

Wood, George H. Winter 1983. "The American Dream, Democracy, and Participatory Theory." *Georgia Social Science Journal* 14: 4–8.

Yankelovich, Skelly, and White, Inc. 1986. *Charitable Behavior of Americans: A National Survey.* Washington, D.C.: Independent Sector.

Zevin, Jack. Spring 1983. "Future Citizens: Children and Politics." *Teaching Political Science* 10: 119–26.

INDEX

Community involvement and volunteering, 31
Community organizations
        collaboration with higher education, 64-65
Compromise bill of 1989, 43
Cooperative Institutional Research Program, 16
"Corporate good citizenship", 25
Corporate sector
        volunteering and philanthropy, 25-26
Council for the Advancement of Citizenship, 38
Council on Adult and Experiential Learning, 52

D
Democratic Leadership Council, 40, 78
Dodd, Christopher, 43
Drew University, 51

E
Education Demonstration Act, 39
Educational Commission of the States, 65, 67
Educational outcomes, 73
        measurement of, 74-75
Educational Testing Service, 63
Experiential education, 58

F
Faculty as role model, 10
Federal work-study program, 16
Financial conditions
        and volunteering, 15
        working students, 15
Florida, University of, West
        health service volunteering, 62
Ford Foundation, 65
Freshmen
        college majors, 16-17
        goals, 17-18
Fund for the Improvement of Postsecondary Education, 63

G
Gallup, George, Jr., 1
Gallup Poll, 48
Georgetown University, 47, 67
Government sector
        as service provider, 26-28
        volunteering and philanthropy, 26
Graduation Equivalency Diploma, 52
Graham, Bob, 43
Great Society, 14, 29

Volunteerism
    definition, 2-3
    factors affecting, 28
    institutional involvement, 6
    minority group concerns, 28-29
    students, 4
Volunteers in Public Schools Program, 63
Volunteers in Service to America, 45

W
Work-study programs, 59

Y
Yale and volunteerism, 67
Youth Community Service, 40
Youth employment programs, 45
Youth Engaged in Service, 44
Youth services
    alternatives to, 51
    college credit for, 52
    educational benefits, 51
    grassroots efforts, 53
Youth Service Corps bill, 42

ASHE-ERIC HIGHER EDUCATION REPORTS

Since 1983, the Association for the Study of Higher Education (ASHE) and the Educational Resources Information Center (ERIC) Clearinghouse on Higher Education, a sponsored project of the School of Education and Human Development at The George Washington University, have cosponsored the *ASHE-ERIC Higher Education Report* series. The 1990 series is the nineteenth overall and the second to be published by the School of Education and Human Development at the George Washington University.

Each monograph is the definitive analysis of a tough higher education problem, based on thorough research of pertinent literature and insitutional experiences. Topics are identified by a national survey. Noted practitioners and scholars are then commissioned to write the reports, with experts providing critical reviews of each manuscript before publication.

Eight monographs (10 before 1985) in the ASHE-ERIC Higher Education Report series are published each year and are available on individual and subscription basis. Subscription to eight issues is $80.00 annually; $60 to members of AAHE, AIR, or AERA; and $50 to ASHE members. All foreign subscribers must include an additional $10 per series year for postage.

To order single copies of existing reports, use the order form on the last page of this book. Regular prices, and special rates available to members of AAHE, AIR, AERA and ASHE, are as follows:

Series	Regular	Members
1990	$17.00	$12.75
1988-89	15.00	11.25
1985-87	10.00	7.50
1983-84	7.50	6.00
before 1983	6.50	5.00

Price includes book rate postage within the U.S. For foreign orders, please add $1.00 per book. Fast United Parcel Service available within the contiguous U.S. at $2.50 for each order under $50.00, and calculated at 5% of invoice total for orders $50.00 or above.

All orders under $45.00 must be prepaid. Make check payable to ASHE-ERIC. For Visa or MasterCard, include card number, expiration date and signature. A bulk discount of 10% is available on orders of 15 or more books (not applicable on subscriptions).

Address order to
  ASHE-ERIC Higher Education Reports
  The George Washington University
  1 Dupont Circle, Suite 630
  Washington, DC 20036
Or phone (202) 296-2597
  Write or call for a complete catalog of ASHE-ERIC Higher Education Reports.

1990 ASHE-ERIC Higher Education Reports

1. The Campus Green: Fund Raising in Higher Education
   Barbara E. Brittingham and Thomas R. Pezzullo

2. The Emeritus Professor: Old Rank - New Meaning
   James E. Mauch, Jack W. Birch, and Jack Matthews

3. "High Risk" Students in Higher Education: Future Trends
   Dionne J. Jones and Betty Collier Watson

4. Budgeting for Higher Education at the State Level: Enigma,
   Paradox, and Ritual
   Daniel T. Layzell and Jan W. Lyddon

5. Proprietary Schools: Programs, Policies, and Prospects
   John B. Lee and Jamie P. Merisotis

6. College Choice: Understanding Student Enrollment Behavior
   Michael B. Paulsen

7. Pursuing Diversity: Recruiting College Minority Students
   Barbara Astone and Elsa Nuñez-Wormack

1989 ASHE-ERIC Higher Education Reports

1. Making Sense of Administrative Leadership: The 'L' Word in
   Higher Education
   Estela M. Bensimon, Anna Neumann, and Robert Birnbaum

2. Affirmative Rhetoric, Negative Action: African-American and
   Hispanic Faculty at Predominantly White Universities
   Valora Washington and William Harvey

3. Postsecondary Developmental Programs: A Traditional Agenda
   with New Imperatives
   Louise M. Tomlinson

4. The Old College Try: Balancing Athletics and Academics in
   Higher Education
   John R. Thelin and Lawrence L. Wiseman

5. The Challenge of Diversity: Involvement or Alienation in the
   Academy?
   Daryl G. Smith

6. Student Goals for College and Courses: A Missing Link in Assess-
   ing and Improving Academic Achievement
   Joan S. Stark, Kathleen M. Shaw, and Malcolm A. Lowther

7. The Student as Commuter: Developing a Comprehensive Institutional Response
   Barbara Jacoby

8. Renewing Civic Capacity: Preparing College Students for Service
   and Citizenship
   Suzanne W. Morse

1988 ASHE-ERIC Higher Education Reports

1. The Invisible Tapestry: Culture in American Colleges and Universities
   George D. Kuh and Elizabeth J. Whitt

2. Critical Thinking: Theory, Research, Practice, and Possibilities
   Joanne Gainen Kurfiss

3. Developing Academic Programs: The Climate for Innovation
   Daniel T. Seymour

4. Peer Teaching: To Teach is To Learn Twice
   Neal A. Whitman

5. Higher Education and State Governments: Renewed Partnership, Cooperation, or Competition?
   Edward R. Hines

6. Entrepreneurship and Higher Education: Lessons for Colleges, Universities, and Industry
   James S. Fairweather

7. Planning for Microcomputers in Higher Education: Strategies for the Next Generation
   Reynolds Ferrante, John Hayman, Mary Susan Carlson, and Harry Phillips

8. The Challenge for Research in Higher Education: Harmonizing Excellence and Utility
   Alan W. Lindsay and Ruth T. Neumann

1987 ASHE-ERIC Higher Education Reports

1. Incentive Early Retirement Programs for Faculty: Innovative Responses to a Changing Environment
   Jay L. Chronister and Thomas R. Kepple, Jr.

2. Working Effectively with Trustees: Building Cooperative Campus Leadership
   Barbara E. Taylor

3. Formal Recognition of Employer-Sponsored Instruction: Conflict and Collegiality in Postsecondary Education
   Nancy S. Nash and Elizabeth M. Hawthorne

4. Learning Styles: Implications for Improving Educational Practices
   Charles S. Claxton and Patricia H. Murrell

5. Higher Education Leadership: Enhancing Skills through Professional Development Programs
   Sharon A. McDade

6. Higher Education and the Public Trust: Improving Stature in Colleges and Universities
   Richard L. Alfred and Julie Weissman

---

7. College Student Outcomes Assessment: A Talent Development Perspective
   Maryann Jacobi, Alexander Astin, and Frank Ayala, Jr.

8. Opportunity from Strength: Strategic Planning Clarified with Case Examples
   Robert G. Cope

1986 ASHE-ERIC Higher Education Reports

1. Post-tenure Faculty Evaluation: Threat or Opportunity?
   Christine M. Licata

2. Blue Ribbon Commissions and Higher Education: Changing Academe from the Outside
   Janet R. Johnson and Laurence R. Marcus

3. Responsive Professional Education: Balancing Outcomes and Opportunities
   Joan S. Stark, Malcolm A. Lowther, and Bonnie M.K. Hagerty

4. Increasing Students' Learning: A Faculty Guide to Reducing Stress among Students
   Neal A. Whitman, David C. Spendlove, and Claire H. Clark

5. Student Financial Aid and Women: Equity Dilemma?
   Mary Moran

6. The Master's Degree: Tradition, Diversity, Innovation
   Judith S. Glazer

7. The College, the Constitution, and the Consumer Student: Implications for Policy and Practice
   Robert M. Hendrickson and Annette Gibbs

8. Selecting College and University Personnel: The Quest and the Question
   Richard A. Kaplowitz

1985 ASHE-ERIC Higher Education Reports

1. Flexibility in Academic Staffing: Effective Policies and Practices
   Kenneth P. Mortimer, Marque Bagshaw, and Andrew T. Masland

2. Associations in Action: The Washington, D.C. Higher Education Community
   Harland G. Bloland

3. And on the Seventh Day: Faculty Consulting and Supplemental Income
   Carol M. Boyer and Darrell R. Lewis

4. Faculty Research Performance: Lessons from the Sciences and Social Sciences
   John W. Creswell

5. Academic Program Review: Institutional Approaches, Expectations, and Controversies
   Clifton F. Conrad and Richard F. Wilson

6. Students in Urban Settings: Achieving the Baccalaureate Degree
   Richard C. Richardson, Jr. and Louis W. Bender

7. Serving More Than Students: A Critical Need for College Student Personnel Services
   Peter H. Garland

8. Faculty Participation in Decision Making: Necessity or Luxury?
   Carol E. Floyd

1984 ASHE-ERIC Higher Education Reports

1. Adult Learning: State Policies and Institutional Practices
   K. Patricia Cross and Anne-Marie McCartan

2. Student Stress: Effects and Solutions
   Neal A. Whitman, David C. Spendlove, and Claire H. Clark

3. Part-time Faulty: Higher Education at a Crossroads
   Judith M. Gappa

4. Sex Discrimination Law in Higher Education: The Lessons of the Past Decade. ED 252 169.*
   J. Ralph Lindgren, Patti T. Ota, Perry A. Zirkel, and Nan Van Gieson

5. Faculty Freedoms and Institutional Accountability: Interactions and Conflicts
   Steven G. Olswang and Barbara A. Lee

6. The High Technology Connection: Academic/Industrial Cooperation for Economic Growth
   Lynn G. Johnson

7. Employee Educational Programs: Implications for Industry and Higher Education. ED 258 501.*
   Suzanne W. Morse

8. Academic Libraries: The Changing Knowledge Centers of Colleges and Universities
   Barbara B. Moran

9. Futures Research and the Strategic Planning Process: Implications for Higher Education
   James L. Morrison, William L. Renfro, and Wayne I. Boucher

10. Faculty Workload: Research, Theory, and Interpretation
    Harold E. Yuker

1983 ASHE-ERIC Higher Education Reports

1. The Path to Excellence: Quality Assurance in Higher Education
   Laurence R. Marcus, Anita O. Leone, and Edward D. Goldberg

2. Faculty Recruitment, Retention, and Fair Employment: Obligations and Opportunities
   John S. Waggaman

3. Meeting the Challenges: Developing Faculty Careers. ED 232 516.*
   Michael C.T. Brooks and Katherine L. German

4. Raising Academic Standards: A Guide to Learning Improvement
   Ruth Talbott Keimig

5. Serving Learners at a Distance: A Guide to Program Practices
   Charles E. Feasley

6. Competence, Admissions, and Articulation: Returning to the Basics in Higher Education
   Jean L. Preer

7. Public Service in Higher Education: Practices and Priorities
   Patricia H. Crosson

8. Academic Employment and Retrenchment: Judicial Review and Administrative Action
   Robert M. Hendrickson and Barbara A. Lee

9. Burnout: The New Academic Disease. ED 242 255.*
   Winifred Albizu Melendez and Rafael M. de Guzmán

10. Academic Workplace: New Demands, Heightened Tensions
    Ann E. Austin and Zelda F. Gamson

*Out-of-print. Available through EDRS. Call 1-800-443-ERIC.

Quantity		Amount
_____	Please send a complete set of the 1989 *ASHE-ERIC Higher Education Reports* at $80.00, 33% off the cover price.	_____
_____	Please begin my subscription to the 1990 *ASHE-ERIC Higher Education Reports* at $80.00, 41% off the cover price, starting with Report 1, 1990	_____
_____	Outside the U.S., add $10 per series for postage	_____

Individual reports are avilable at the following prices:

1990 and forward, $17.00	1983 and 1984, $7.50
1988 and 1989, $15.00	1982 and back, $6.50
1985 to 1987, $10.00	

Book rate postage within the U.S. is included. Outside U.S., please add $1 per book for postage. Fast U.P.S. shipping is available within the contiguous U.S. at $2.50 for each order under $50.00, and calculated at 5% of invoice total for orders $50.00 or above. All orders under $45 must be prepaid.

PLEASE SEND ME THE FOLLOWING REPORTS:

Quantity	Report No.	Year	Title	Amount
			Subtotal:	
			Foreign or UPS:	
			Total Due:	

Please check one of the following:

☐ Check enclosed, payable to GWU-ERIC.
☐ Purchase order attached ($45.00 minimum).
☐ Charge my credit card indicated below:
   ☐ Visa   ☐ MasterCard

Expiration Date _____

Name _____

Title _____

Institution _____

Address _____

City _____ State _____ Zip _____

Phone _____

Signature _____ Date _____

SEND ALL ORDERS TO:
ASHE-ERIC Higher Education Reports
The George Washington University
One Dupont Circle, Suite 630
Washington, DC 20036-1183
Phone: (202) 296-2597